Shao-Lin Chuan
The Rhythm and Power
of Tan-Tui

盧瀅如編著

少林拳彈跟

一九九五乙亥年春
舊金山華埠
1995 ©

KUO
SIMMONE

少林拳 弹腿
保健益寿

Shao-Lin Chuan

The Rhythm and Power
of Tan-Tui

Simmone Kuo

North Atlantic Books
Berkeley, California

Shao-Lin Chuan: The Rhythm and Power of Tan-Tui

Published by
North Atlantic Books
P.O. Box 12327
Berkeley, California 94712

Cover design by Leigh McLellan
Book design by Andrea DuFlon

Printed in the United States of America

Distributed to the book trade by Publishers Group West

Shao-Lin Chuan is sponsored by the Society for the Study of Native Arts and Sciences, a nonprofit educational corporation whose goals are to develop an educational and crosscultural perspective linking various scientific, social, and artistic fields; to nurture a holistic view of arts, sciences, humanities, and healing; and to publish and distribute literature on the relationship of mind, body, and nature.

Library of Congress Cataloging-in-Publication Data

Kuo, Simmone.
    Shao-lin chuan: the rhythm and power of tan-tui/Simmone Kuo. p. cm.
    Includes bibliographical references.
    Added title page title: Shao lin ch' üan t' an t' ui.
  –Rhythm and power of tan-tui.
    ISBN 1-55643-229-1 (paper)
    1. Hand-to-hand fighting, Oriental. I. Title. II. Title: Shao lin ch' üan t' an t' ui III.
Title: Rhythm and power of tan-tui
GV 1112.K893 1996
613.6'6–dc20   96-26425
                                                                      CIP

1 2 3 4 5 6 7 8 9 / 00 99 98 97 96

郭師父連蔭

This book is dedicated to Kuo Sifu Lien-Ying.

Promote Culture With Martial Arts[1]

The author at a ceremony for the installation of the Kuo Family plaque
in the Chinese for Affirmative Action Building, San Francisco.

Kuo Lien-Ying

芝蘭自結、山川秀

松柏常留、天地春

"Irises and orchids are in bloom;
mountains and rivers are full of picturesque secnery.
Pine and cypress always remain green; heaven and earth."[2]

Acknowledgments

I am grateful above all to my teacher and late husband Sifu Kuo Lien-Ying for preserving and embodying such a valuable tradition of knowledge. His wish was to transmit that knowledge to the modern world, and his dream was to make Tai-Chi Chuan and Shao-Lin Chuan available in the form of basic physical education. I feel that Sifu joins in my satisfaction that the tradition has taken root in a new generation.

I want to express my lasting appreciation to the many students whose participation and support have contributed, in ways too numerous to mention, to making his dream come true.

Thanks to Jeffrey Kessler, Jonas Hamilton, and Lisa Tomayo for editing, to John Bratten for photography, to Terry Luk (陸潮基) for calligraphy, and to Professor Yao You-Wei (姚有爲) and Jin Yu (金玉) of YangZhou University for the cover painting. Thanks also to the students who assisted in the realization of this project: Dan Wang, Nancy Warner, Renee Wong, Joan Contreras, Chris Shiao, Elise Kazanjian, Daniel Rybold, and Chhoury Yam.

— *Simmone Kuo*

Contents

Preface

As a kinesiologist, I have always been impressed with the knowledge and history that can be expressed in a movement form. I am intrigued by the idea that a culture's age-old wisdom can be transmitted through movement. I imagine that centuries of refinement must have preceded the development of the precise movement forms that today embody both Tai-Chi Chuan and Shao-Lin Chuan. To me, these complementary systems are an expression of the unity of form and function.

The movement forms, when performed correctly, accomplish the goal of harmoniously developing strength and flexibility, speed and slowness control, balance and explosive directional movement. The practice of the internal and external systems of Tai-Chi Chuan and Shao-Lin Chuan encourages inward focus on the part of the performer, and an increase in kinesthetic awareness (a sense of one's position and movement in space). You cannot practice these forms without a good deal of self-reflection.

From my perspective, it is this coupling of self-reflection and physical control in the practice of the art that leads to the development of self-knowledge, a sense of presence and confidence, and skill over the precise control of the body in space and time.

I have studied with Simmone Kuo at San Francisco State University since my arrival on campus in 1991 as the Chair of the Department of Kinesiology. My experience in both sport and dance and my scholarly interest in the study of human movement attracted me to her classes. I had always wanted to study Tai-Chi Chuan and was looking forward to the experience of completely immersing myself in movement. Two years later, I encouraged Simmone to develop a course in Shao-Lin Chuan Tan-Tui. She had often spoken of this external form, of its significance, and of its complementarity to Tai-Chi Chuan. As Department Chair, I was and remain interested in offering a well-rounded program in the Asian martial arts and was particularly interested in noncombative forms. Once the course was developed, I knew that I had to study Shao-Lin Chuan.

I find Shao-Lin Chuan to be invigorating and challenging. I love the speed and fluidity that the movement offers and the tremendous sense of satisfaction one achieves in being able to complete the ten lines continuously.

I am delighted that the Tan-Tui forms are now committed to this book. It will enable me to mentally review and study these forms at my leisure. I find this very useful, even when knowing the movement, because each reading is done anew and seems to result in fresh insights that enhance my performance.

—*Susan Higgins, Professor and Chair, Department of Kinesiology,*
San Francisco State University

June 1993

榮獲揚州師範大學武術教授

Simmone Kuo receives the honorary title of Professor, YangZhou University,
YangZhou City, China

On the Stork Tower

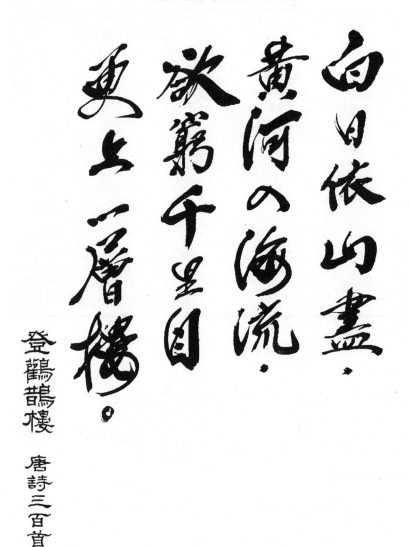

白日依山盡，
黃河入海流。
欲窮千里目，
更上一層樓。

登鸛鵲樓　唐詩三百首

The sun beyond the mountains glows;
The Yellow River seaward flows.
You can enjoy a grander sight
By climbing to a greater height.[3]

Foreword

When I first came to the Lien-Ying Tai-Chi Chuan Academy in 1977, Simu (Master) Kuo explained that it was customary for young boys to begin by studying Shao-Lin Chuan. She explained that the rapid, direct, and forceful movements of Shao-Lin Chuan boxing are suited to the high energy levels of children, helping to keep them calm and well-behaved. I cannot say whether or not Shao-Lin Chuan improved my behavior; it certainly was a great adventure for an eleven-year-old. Sifu Kuo was still alive, and who can forget the magnanimous way he walked among the many students who filled Chinatown's Portsmouth Square, capable of the most acrobatic steps even at an advanced age? Simu Kuo instructed me in the first three lines of the form called Tan-Tui (or "Springy Legs"), the foundation of Shao-Lin Chuan.

Even then, the proud postures and graceful movements of this form made a certain impression, though I did not fully understand or appreciate Shao-Lin Chuan's potential benefits. My strength, balance, and coordination improved considerably, only the most obvious manifestations of practice. Since that distant time, these exercises have sustained me in various endeavors, including teaching and graduate study. A fine teacher of Tan-Tui, Simu Kuo has always emphasized the potential benefits of Shao-Lin Chuan and Tai-Chi Chuan in personal and professional life. Tan-Tui, in keeping with its name, can serve as a springboard for other creative endeavors. Many have realized this possibility through Simu Kuo's example and the dedication of her senior students. Shao-Lin Chuan Tan-Tui has "set my feet upon a rock, making my steps secure," and is a source of great vigor, dexterity, and even peace of mind to anyone able to practice it regularly.

—*Jonas Hamilton*
Graduate Student, History Department, Columbia University

The Kuo Family and students from China.

Foreword II

I have been asked by my teacher Simmone Kuo to compose a short perspective on Shao-Lin Chuan, a martial art form that I have been studying with her for several years. Like all good fortune, my coming to know Simmone followed a certain path. I had been studying Tai-Chi Chuan for three years and was talking with my friend, Curtis Chong, about the benefits of it in my life. He began studying Tai-Chi Chuan with Simmone. Later he introduced me to Simmone and she has been my teacher since that time.

Shao-Lin means "youth," and *Chuan* means "fist." Thus, Shao-Lin Chuan means "martial art for the young." I was forty-seven years old when I started. Simu Kuo initially had some reservations about teaching me Shao-Lin Chuan, and planned to teach me only the first two lines of the form. I started in October and had learned the first two lines by the time Simmone left in December for a vacation. When I returned to class in January, she was pleasantly surprised! She had thought that I might have forgotten the two lines and "The fist for youth" dictum would be proved. Instead she found that I still knew the lines and that my body and I had improved. Since that time we have continued working as a team. As an older student, I could follow more easily the dictum of the Lien-Ying Academy: *"Practice, Practice Every Day: Miss One Day, Lose Ten Days; No Hurry, No Slack: A Well-Paced Practice Is The Way To Success."* Combining Shao-Lin Chuan with Tai-Chi Chuan has allowed me to develop my mind, body, and spirit. Every day, my muscles gain in strength and flexibility, which is a great feeling as one confronts the aging process.

—*Geoffrey Shaskan*

The Kuo Family was invited to participate in the movie The Killer Elite *in 1974.*

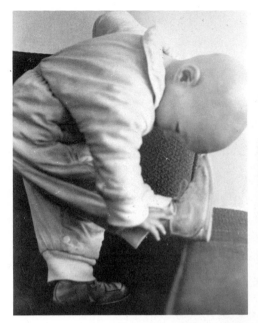 

郭中美 *Chung-Mei Kuo*
inspired all the students from an early age.

萬里傳道
千秋受益

*Use the doctrines of ancient sages to benefit mankind
for thousands of years.*[4]

Introduction to the Kuo Family

Simmone (Simu) Kuo is a master of Tai-Chi Chuan, Shao-Lin Chuan, Shing-Yi Chuan, Pa-Kua Tsang, the staff, the broadsword, and the Tai-Chi Sword. She is currently the instructor at the Lien-Ying Tai-Chi Chuan Academy at 15-A Walter U. Lum Place in San Francisco, California. Since 1980, she has also served on the Kinesiology Department faculty at San Francisco State University, teaching Tai-Chi Chuan and Shao-Lin Chuan. In 1975, she wrote and performed a series of television programs that was broadcast nationally.

Mrs. Kuo's husband, the late Kuo Lien-Ying, was an international figure in the martial arts community. A living legend, Sifu Kuo was a practitioner of the arts for more than seventy years. He taught the traditional style of Tai-Chi Chuan that has been handed down through the ages. Sifu Kuo was also a congressman in the National Assembly of China in Taiwan and mainland China.

Sifu and Simu Kuo have one son, Chung-Mei, born in 1967, who began practicing Tai-Chi Chuan and Shao-Lin Chuan as soon as he could walk.

Few teachers of Tai-Chi Chuan can match Simu Kuo's energy, simplicity, and clarity of style. Simu's constant efforts to improve and demystify this art have earned her a growing popularity. She has been very successful in interpreting Tai-Chi Chuan for Americans through television, publications, and numerous classes in colleges, universities, and other educational institutions.

In 1977, the Chinese Culture Foundation presented a series of multicultural training programs for secondary school teachers that reached thirty-six schools under a project of the Office of Education of the City of San Francisco. When we approached Simu to teach Tai-Chi Chuan, she was enthusiastic and generously shared with us her accumulated experience, knowledge, and materials. Upon completion of the training session, a *Teacher's Handbook on Tai-Chi Chuan* was produced that was so popular that it quickly sold out. In 1991, a much-expanded version of that book called *Long Life, Good Health through Tai-Chi Chuan* was published by North Atlantic Books, so that many more people have been able to benefit both spiritually and physically from this ancient and enduring Chinese physical art form.

We are, therefore, greatly pleased that Simu is now publishing this companion volume in order to share her knowledge of the complementary martial art Shao-Lin Chuan Tan-Tui with the Western public.

— Dr. Shirley Sun
Former Executive Director, Chinese Culture Foundation

Author's Introduction

This book on Shao-Lin Chuan Tan-Tui is like a textbook; we use words that are easy to understand and accompany them with clear photographs. Like its companion volume *Long Life, Good Health through Tai-Chi Chuan,* this book is intended as a resource for both students and teachers of traditional Chinese martial arts. Tan-Tui, the introductory set of Shao-Lin Chuan, is a very easy form to learn. It takes about thirty hours to learn in its entirety, consists of ten lines, and takes approximately fifteen minutes to perform. The Tan-Tui movements and choreography are beautiful, and extremely aerobic.

Shao-Lin Chuan has more than 360 different sets. Tan-Tui is the beginning set, which includes punching, kicking, crouching, and leaping. This form helps the student build body strength and gain flexibility and concentration. After having learned and practiced the ten lines of Tan-Tui for some time, the student may then be ready for more advanced Shao-Lin Chuan forms like Tsa-Chuan and Erh-Lang Chuan, which require greater energy and strength.

As a twelve-year-old youth in Inner Mongolia, Sifu Kuo began his study of the martial arts with Shao-Lin Chuan Tan-Tui. He always retained a particular fondness for this rigorous set of Shao-Lin Chuan fundamentals. Sifu Kuo went on to master a variety of martial arts, while also exploring the practices of the world's different religious traditions. In addition to being one of the most esteemed and accomplished martial artists of his generation, Sifu Kuo was a Congressman in the National Assembly of China, initially in mainland China, then in Taiwan. He moved to San Francisco in 1965 and established the Lien-Ying Tai-Chi Chuan Martial Arts Academy. Since that time, the Academy has been a center for practice and training in the traditional martial arts of China (Tai-Chi Chuan, Shao-Lin Chuan, Shing-Yi Chuan, Pa-Kua Tsang, etc.).

Sifu Kuo strongly recommended that all students study the forms of both Tai-Chi Chuan, which is an "internal" system, and Shao-Lin Chuan, which is an "external" system. (Internal: The speed is slower and balanced; punching or pushing is softer; using mainly the palms. External: Faster; punching harder; using mainly the fists.) This is because the body needs both internal and external exercise to remain balanced. After learning Tai-Chi Chuan, which is a slower, more meditative set of movements, students usually notice that their joints are very stiff. Learning the Tan-Tui set limbers up the student's body and joints after a few months. Daily practice of the Shao-Lin Chuan Tan-Tui form will help the student feel refreshed and full of energy.

Please see the back of this book for photographs of Sifu Kuo performing related martial art forms, which also come from the legacy of Shao-Lin Chuan.

Origins of Chinese Martial Arts

The history of Chinese martial arts is known primarily through oral tradition handed down by successive generations of teachers to their closest students. Some documents and pictorial representations exist from nearly 2,000 years ago, but the actual origins of the martial arts are prehistoric and remain shrouded in legend. (See the next chapter, "The Wu-Shu Records in the Tun-Huang Mo Kao K'u Caves.")

According to Sifu Kuo, the martial arts grew naturally out of human beings' need to secure and defend territory for living space. The fighting forms that existed in every part of China at the dawn of history are said to have grown out of human beings' ability not only to understand the natural world, but to appreciate and enter into a sort of sympathetic resonance with all natural phenomena. The early martial artists devised new ways of holding and moving their bodies by pondering the physical properties of nature: the operation of elemental forces like wind; the positional energy and balance of rocks; the growth and resilience of trees; the movements of animals in attack and defense.

The resulting forms of movement were gathered into sets or routines and gradually refined. In some cases, the outer form of movement has been directly imitated—stepping and pouncing like a cat, for example. In others, it is more the spirit or the essence of a way of moving—for instance, continuously falling like water—that has been embodied and developed.

The first weapons consisted of natural objects such as sticks and stones. With the development of human culture and technology, people began to fashion more durable and menacing weapons, using tempered metal to form swords, spears, and so on.

The early martial artists discovered that their practice, when conducted in a careful and intensive manner, resulted not only in superior fighting skills but also in overall good health and an abundance of energy, alertness, and capacity for concentration. This discovery is the basis for *wu-shu* (*wu*, "martial," *shu*, "skill," "act"), the special skill of the martial arts, and explains the reverence Chinese people have always felt for the martial arts. These arts are understood not only as an excellent system for training in direct combat, but also as a way to health and inner development, through cultivation of a harmony that comprises all aspects of the individual—body, mind, and spirit.

The Legacy Of Shao-Lin Chuan

Shao-Lin Temple is honored throughout the world as the source of the distinctive Chinese martial arts tradition. It was here, through an encounter with Buddhism, that the numerous and varied native fighting forms of China were refined into a system that has thrived for 1,500 years. Before the Shao-Lin Temple period (500 C.E.), the martial arts had long been influenced by both Taoist and Confucian ideals. (See the chapter entitled "Chinese Philosophy and Religion Related to Shao-Lin Chuan.") The fighting forms were still somewhat wild, tending toward violence and purely pragmatic application in battle. Through the development of Shao-Lin Chuan, Chinese martial arts became a philosophically based system oriented toward health, exercise, and inner development.

During the fifth century C.E., the Buddhist monk Ta-Mo (Bodhidharma) made a pilgrimage from his native India to China. He made his way to an isolated Buddhist monastery in central China's Honan Province. Today this monastery is known as Shao-Lin (Forest of Youth) Temple. Here Ta-Mo taught for many years. The monks who lived there, chanting in prayer, seemed listless and lacking in both physical energy and alertness. Ta-Mo began teaching them Indian yoga exercises and Chan meditation (*Chan* 禪 = "meditation," Zen in Japanese, from the Sanskrit *dhyana*), in order to help them reconnect with the wellsprings of energy and consciousness in their own bodies.

At the temple lived a group of eighteen monks who spent their youth in a criminal gang and had come to the temple in remorse, seeking a better way of life. These monks, who had formerly used their skill in martial arts for unjust purposes, now began to practice *wu-shu* again together with Ta-Mo's exercises and meditation. They became so famous throughout China for their good deeds and energetic public service that today they are considered *lohans* (superhuman heroes). The eighteen monks serve as inspirational examples for young people of the great benefits that come from redirecting chaotic and violent energy to personal development and the common good.

The system of Shao-Lin Chuan grew out of this blending of yoga exercises and meditation with the native fighting forms of China, giving a whole new direction to the martial arts. This approach to martial arts is a form of moving meditation, seeking to combine physical, mental, and spiritual disciplines into a single practice. Generations of Shao-Lin monks have distinguished themselves in battle as embodiments of a fierce fighting spirit. At the same time, these consummate martial artists have preserved the rich tradition of martial arts practice as a way to health and inner harmony.

The fortuitous interaction of cultures and traditions that occurred at Shao-Lin Temple many centuries ago has brought forth great knowledge. Ta-Mo is the founder and first patriarch of Chan Buddhism. This form of Buddhism spread from China to Korea and Japan, then to the rest of the world. Similarly, the tradition of classical Chinese martial arts, including Shao-Lin Chuan and Tai-Chi Chuan, spread from Shao-Lin Temple first to other Asian countries, then throughout the world.

Gate of Shao-Lin Temple.

北魏古刹 禅宗祖庭

武術

Shao-Lin Temple abbot (center) and disciples.

武術

This is the martial arts from the eighteen monks of Shao-Lin Temple.

The Wu-Shu Records in the Tun-Huang Mo Kao K'u Caves

The Tun-Huang Mo Kao K'u Caves are home to one of the greatest *wu-shu* art museums in the world. Tun-Huang ("Blazing Sun") was the border oasis town and gateway to China from Central Asia. The Tun-Huang Cave complex is one of the oldest Chinese cave temples, with elaborate religious scenes sculpted into the living rock on a grand scale. Artistically, the Tun-Huang Caves span seven imperial dynasties and approximately ten centuries, from the fourth through fourteenth centuries C.E. More than 480 carvings in a variety of sizes were cut into the rock to serve as testimony to the glory of Buddha and his teachings, and the vigor of his followers.

From the time of the Han dynasty (100 C.E.) to the present, the Tun-Huang Caves have been important politically, commercially, and militarily. The caves are positioned along the "Silk Road" in China, a strategic location which resulted in their also being used as a military base.

The caves at Tun-Huang and at the Tun-Huang National Art Research Institute were evaluated in the 1980s by *wu-shu* experts. Their research uncovered a large hidden section of sixty-one caves with carvings of entire martial arts sets in order of performance. The figures are even named. There is a "Strength Contest" picture in the Scripture Cave, a "Wrestling" carving in Cave #290, a Tang dynasty "Pair-Up Exercise" in Cave #195, the "Hercules Holding Show" in Cave #249, and "Swordsmanship" in Cave #61. These postures show new styles of boxing and wrestling, as well as swordsmanship, riding and shooting, and spear and shield fighting. They are skillfully drawn to approximate real combat situations.

The Tun-Huang Caves are a valuable resource for martial artists because of their systematic depiction of combat technique, as well as a textbook for advanced study by the martial arts student. The Tun-Huang Caves are open to the public and provide a valuable resource for learning about Chinese history.

Gate of Tun-Huang.

Caves of Tun-Huang.

故人入夢
長相思憶

Knowing how much I think of you always,
Into my dreams, so you did make your ways.[5]
"Dreaming of Li Bai"

Benefits

The development of deep, smooth breathing is one of the biggest challenges and greatest benefits of Shao-Lin Chuan Tan-Tui practice. Since the breath serves as a nexus between the outer and the inner, between the voluntary and involuntary functions of the body, correct breathing has the effect of harmonizing body, mind, and spirit.

When Shao-Lin Chuan Tan-Tui is practiced correctly, it can bring increased strength, stamina, and overall flexibility. Another benefit is the strengthening of the cardiovascular system. Better breathing and heart function help to balance the different body systems and enhance overall health. As relaxation of the breath through mindful and rhythmic movement harmonizes the body and mind, awareness naturally expands. This awareness radiates out into the world through the student's relationships, work, and other activities.

Martial arts practice is renowned for developing personal confidence and a greater sense of presence, and is particularly useful for performing artists of all kinds. (See, for example, the chapter entitled "Beijing Opera and Chinese Acrobatics".) Martial arts practice can help people deal with health problems and imbalances in a realistic and effective manner. Practice can also be viewed as a process of reeducation therapy: through perseverance it is possible to renew the whole person.

Preparatory Notes

Shao-Lin Chuan forms like Tan-Tui are traditionally practiced primarily by young people (in America beginning at age twelve; in China, children begin at age six). However, thirty years of teaching at the Lien-Ying Tai-Chi Chuan Academy of San Francisco have demonstrated that Tan-Tui practice can also be beneficial for middle-aged and more elderly persons, especially when combined with the practice of Tai-Chi Chuan. The external and internal forms are complementary, with one focusing on outer strength and stamina, the other on inner strength and flexibility. Given the sedentary, at times overly mental life-style of many modern people, regular exercise is necessary for physical health and overall balance. No matter what the student's age or initial physical condition, flexibility, strength, and aerobic conditioning can be gradually developed.

Tan-Tui is best practiced in loose-fitting, layered clothing and flat shoes. In cold weather one should consider wearing a hat and gloves. It is important that the body be kept warm both during and after practice. It is suggested that both men and women wear some type of support around the waist and upper hips during practice. Women should wear a sports bra and control-top underwear. Women should not practice as vigorously during menstruation.

An open outdoor space of at least ten feet by fifteen to twenty feet is best, and early morning is the ideal time for practice. However, an indoor space is adequate, and it is possible to practice at any time, except within an hour after a large meal. Silence should be maintained during and after practice in order for the student to begin to develop concentration. It is best to breathe through the nose, unless there is congestion. The number of repetitions in each of the ten lines can be varied according to the constraints of space and time, as well as the stamina of the student.

Direct instruction from a qualified teacher is essential. To learn even the outline of the movements from a book or video is very difficult. A teacher is necessary to guide the student into a balanced and fruitful practice. At certain points, the student may need to relax or slow down; at others, to exert more force and speed up. Working with a good teacher will help the student avoid injuries and derive maximum benefit from practice.

Although association with a teacher is important, in the end, the student is creating his/her own experience. The teacher can only guide the student toward greater balance within the context of that experience. The teacher/student relationship in martial arts is different from that in Western education, where the student generally expects the teacher to answer his/her questions. In martial arts practice, the teacher guides the student deeper and deeper into his/her own experience, to find his/her own answers and still deeper questions.

A standard schedule for Shao-Lin Chuan Tan-Tui, with one lesson per week, is to introduce new movements every other week. On the "off" week, the lesson is devoted to practice and refinement of details. Such a schedule assumes that the student practices regularly on his/her own between lessons.

The teacher must pay attention to each individual student's capabilities. Issues of flexibility and stamina are important, and lessons must take into account any particular limitations. For those with joint problems, the lowering-down movements and kicks may be somewhat modified for comfort and safety. Elderly persons and those with compromised health can benefit from learning and practicing only the warm-up exercises or, at most, only the lines with no lowering-down (lines 2, 3, 4, 5, 9).

In any case, consistent and diligent practice is needed in order to gain the many benefits of Shao-Lin Chuan Tan-Tui.

Difficulties

It is important to follow the rule of progressing from the easy to the difficult. For example, with the kicking movements, beginners should start off with a low, light, and slow movement, increasing height, force, and speed progressively. Untrained individuals should be especially careful to go step by step and refrain from overexertion in performing high and swift kicks. The chin to toe exercise is another challenge, requiring proper body and foot positions. The force used in stretching should be increased gradually as the student becomes stronger and more skillful. Moreover, it is important that breathing remain relaxed and smooth, especially during difficult exercises and movements. Practicing the various exercises regularly will help strengthen the student's abilities as well as improve execution of the form. It is good to practice with at least one other person or a group whenever possible so that each student can help correct the other.

When the student first begins doing the strenuous exercises and movements, the muscles may be quite sore, especially in the lower limbs. This is normal. To ease the soreness, a student should always do warm-up exercises before each session and then light exercises to relax the muscles afterward. Massaging or applying a hot compress can also provide relief. After a period of regular practice, the student's flexibility will improve and the pain will dissipate.

Correct posture is very important and should always be kept in mind. In the beginning when the student performs frontal kicks, the foot may not reach the height of his/her forehead. It is preferable to kick lower, just above waist level, and keep the back and leg straight and the torso erect. Once the student develops a habit of executing kicks or other movements improperly, such habits can be very difficult to correct. This in turn will hamper long-term development.

When practicing, the student should strive for harmony among the movements of the hands, feet, body, and eyes. Always attempt to exert force smoothly rather than in jerky motions. Correct breathing is also very important. Air should be inhaled through the nose while the mouth is kept closed. Proper breathing creates a higher level of *chi* (氣), movement of the breath in the body, that helps to promote overall good health.

Sifu Kuo always stressed that if a student is not feeling well on a particular day, he/she should not hesitate to practice. In fact, the student should make sure that a lot of practice is done on that day. Thus the student helps his/her body regain what it has lost. On the other hand, if a student does feel well on a specific day, he/she need not practice as much, since there are no negative feelings or energy needing to be discarded. In any case, it is important to practice every day.

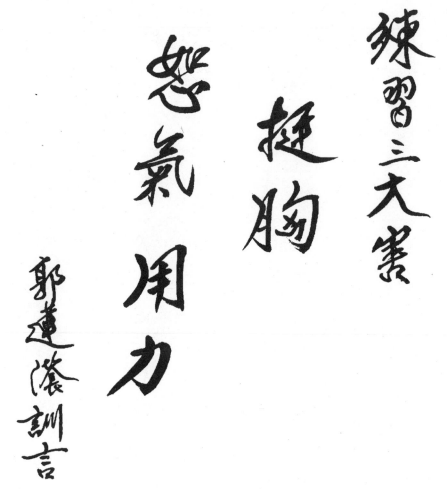

The three things to avoid in the practice of Shao-Lin Chuan are:

> *Thrusting out of the chest*
> *Hold the chest naturally (not with tension or jerky movements).*
>
> *Forcefully expelling the breath*
> *For vitality breathe naturally.*
>
> *Overextending one's strength*
> *Strength is borrowed from the opponent.*
>
> *—The teaching of Master Kuo Lien-Ying*

Shao-Lin Chuan
Basic Warm-Up Exercises for Tan-Tui

1. Rotating Waist

2. Rotating Hip

3. Rotating Knee

4. Palm to Floor

5. Side Leg Stretch

6. Chin to Toe

7. Diagonal Kick

8. Straight Kick (Toe Flexed and Toe Pointed)

9. Hand Slapping Foot Kick

10. Double Kick

To find the essence of Shao-Lin Chuan,
one must develop patience and perserverance.
This will lead to the finding of inner truth.
—The teaching of Master Kuo Lien-Ying

柔腰
1. Rotating Waist

Stand straight, with feet together, hands on waist, and fingers pointing toward each other at the small of the back. The thumbs are forward, the four fingers on the back. Use fingers to push the stomach forward, and start rotating the hips in circles: thirty-two times to the right, and thirty-two times to the left.

Note
Keep the knees straight, but not locked. This exercise aids digestion and strengthens the waist and stomach muscles.

A   B

柔跨

2. Rotating Hip

Stand straight with feet parallel and one foot length apart. Put the hands on the lower hips, with fingers towards the back and pointing down. The thumbs are forward, the four fingers on the back of the hip. Use the left hand to push the hip toward the right, and rotate hips in an oval movement backward thirty-two times. Repeat thirty-two times towards the left.

Note
This exercise helps loosen the hip joints.

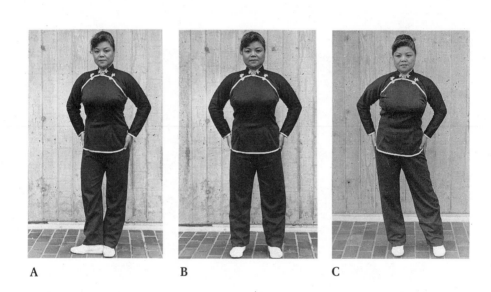

A   B   C

柔膝

3. Rotating Knee

Stand straight, with feet together and knees bent. Put the hands on the knees, with fingers open and elbows straight. Keep the back straight and the chin up. In the beginning, rotate the knees in a circular motion six times to the right, and then six times to the left. This exercise is hard to do, but try to work up to twenty rotations in each direction by the end of one month, and thirty-two by the end of two months. When finished, use the palms to push the knees straight back, keeping the back straight and the chin up, and stay in this position for one minute.

Note
It is important to keep the knees bent and the elbows straight while exercising. This exercise strengthens the ankle and knee joints and aids in balance.

A   B   C

手心貼地
4. Palm to Floor

Stand straight, feet together, chin up, and arms extended overhead. Clasp fingers with palms facing the sky. Lean first to one side, then the other, keeping the elbows straight. Do this three times to stretch the sides of the chest and arms. Then, still keeping the elbows and knees straight, bend forward as far as possible, keeping the back straight. After some practice, it will be easy to touch the ground with the palms or even with the elbows; but in the beginning, do not force the palms down. Instead, bounce gently up and down to stretch the back muscles.

Note
It is important not to force the palms to the floor. It is more important to do this exercise correctly, with the back straight; touching the ground will come naturally. Remember to keep the knees straight and the head up. This exercise stretches the muscles of the sides and back.

A   B

C   D   E

仆腿
5. Side Leg Stretch

Spread legs with knees bent, feet parallel, approximately two shoulder widths apart, and hands on the knees. The knees are noticeably bent, and the body is slightly forward. Then, bend the right knee as far as possible while rotating the body to the left, keeping the feet parallel. This exercise stretches the inner leg. Do the same for the right leg, bending the left knee and rotating the body to the right.

Note
It is important to remember that this is a very difficult exercise to do properly. Do not force the stretching. In the beginning it is permissible to hold on for support.

B   A   B

C2   C1

C3   C4

J. Russell Gabel.

Sonia V. Gabel.

Sonia V. Gabel.

John J. Hannon.

Never too old, never too young to study.

Mariana Tiley practices Shao-Lin Chuan.

J. Russell Gabel.

少林拳

北京通縣 *Students from Beijing Tung County.*

金鶏啄食
6. Chin to Toe

This exercise used to be called "Golden Cock Pecking at Food." Stand straight, with feet together and the left foot turned 45 degrees outward. Step forward with the right foot approximately two feet, with heel down and toes up. All the weight is on the back foot. Bend forward from the waist, keeping the right leg straight and the left leg bent, and put both hands on the right knee. If you can, reach down with both hands and pull back the right foot. As you stretch, keep the chin up. Then do the same for the left leg. Step forward with the left foot, bend forward, and put both hands on the left knee. In the beginning, simply bounce the body up and down several times, stretching the leg tendons. After a year or more of practice it will be possible to touch the chin to the toe. However, do not force the body into this position.

A
C
B

J. Russell Gabel.

Sonia V. Gabel.

Simu Kuo, Chin to Toe, in 1968. At that time
she started teaching.

Note

It is very important to practice these exercises every day. They will make the body feel good and limber up the muscles, tendons, and joints. It is more important to do the exercises continually and properly than to strain in any one of them.

In the old days, students had to put chin to toe before learning the first step of Shao-Lin Chuan or Tai-Chi Chuan. Today students can begin learning the forms right away, but chin to toe is still part of the license for teaching.

左右十字腿
7. Diagonal Kick

Stand straight with both hands on the small of the back, thumbs forward, four fingers back, and feet together. Step forward 45 degrees to the left side with the left foot (A). As soon as the left foot steps forward, continue in one motion to kick in the same diagonal direction with the right foot, keeping the knee straight and foot up (B). End by bringing the right foot back to the left foot arch. Now do the reverse step 45 degrees to the right side with the right foot (C). Kick with the left foot diagonally to the right side, bringing it back to the right foot arch (D). Repeat six to twelve times.

Note
It is important to keep the hands on the small of the back, to keep the back straight, and to look in front while kicking. In the beginning, do not kick too high.

A B

C D

踢勾腿
8. Straight Kick (Toe Flexed and Toe Pointed)

Stand straight with both hands at center of back and feet together. Take a small step with the right foot (A) and kick straight up with the left foot, keeping the knee straight and the toes pointed up (B). During the downward portion of the kick, flex the ankle to extend the toes forward. End with the left toes touching the ground slightly in front of the body (C), then take a small step with the same foot, and kick with the right foot (D). Repeat kicks six to twelve times.

Note
Do not force the kicks, especially in the beginning. It is not important to kick very high.

A   B

C   D

踢拍平腿
9. Hand Slapping Foot Kick

Stand straight with the feet together and hands to the sides, making fists at chest level. Take a small step with the right foot (A) and kick forward with the left foot. At the same time, open and extend the left hand, letting the hand and foot meet in front and making a slapping sound (B). Bring the left hand back to its original position and end the kick with the left toe touching the floor slightly in front (C). Now take a small step with the left foot, and repeat for the right side, kicking with the right leg and slapping the right foot with the right hand (D). Continue for six to twelve kicks.

Note
Keep the knees straight and the feet extended when kicking. Do not force the slapping motions.

A   B

C   D

二起脚
10. Double Kick

Bring the right fist forward; the heel of the right foot is up, the knees are bent, and the weight is on the left foot (A). Take a small step forward with the right foot, and lift up the left knee and fist. Pull back the right fist (B). Then spring up on and kick with the right leg, hitting the foot with the extended right hand before the left foot touches down on the ground. The left fist is pulled back to the left side during the "springing up." Now perform the exercise on the other side, substituting right for left and vice versa.

Note
Do not force this movement. Practice it many times before going further. People over forty years of age usually do not jump, but simply raise their foot and hit it with the hand (C).

A   B   C

Supplementary Exercises

HEEL KICK

GOLDEN POST STANCE

Examples of Palm and Fist Hand Forms in Tan-Tui Ten Lines

OPEN PALM

HAND STANDING PUNCH

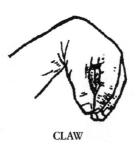

FLAT PUNCH

CLAW

Supplementary Kicking Exercises

Supplementary Kicking Exercises

Arm Rotation Exercise

Take the bow-and-arrow stance with the left foot in front and the right foot in back. Place the left hand on the left side waist. Rotate the right arm from right shoulder, across the left shoulder, over the left knee and repeat. (Don't overextend the arm back past the shoulder and keep your fingers straight.) Repeat this motion twelve times. Then do the exercise in reverse twelve times (rotate the right arm from right shoulder, over the left knee, and then across the left shoulder). Repeat the whole exercise for the left arm.

The Arm Rotation Exercise promotes relaxation of the shoulders, neck, and chest. It also helps to improve breathing, reduce stress, and reduce feelings of anger. Students, computer operators, and others can benefit from this exercise.

Stretch on Great Wall in Beijing, 1993.

A

*A beginning student would
need six months to one year
to feel comfortable in
this position.*

B

*The next exercise would take an intermediate
student one to two years to feel comfortable
in this position.*

C

*The last exercise would take an advanced
student at least two years to feel comfortable
in this position.*

Shao-Lin Chuan Tan-Tui at San Francisco State University.

弓字腿 *Bow-And-Arrow Stance*
The bow-and-arrow stance is part of the basic training for Shao-Lin Chuan Tan-Tui
students. With this exercise, students develop precise balance and flexibility.

馬步 *Horse Stance*
In olden days students were required to stand for
hours in the horse stance in order to develop
strength and balance, especially for horseback
riding. Now, since we use cars instead of horses,
students stand in this position for 15-30 minutes.

Shao-Lin Chuan Tan-Tui at San Francisco State University.

揚州師大體育系 *Students at YangZhou University.*

少林拳彈腿

Shao-Lin Chuan Tan-Tui
The Ten Lines of Springy Legs

1. Tiger Grasping the Head

2. Reverse Cartwheel

3. Strike with a Forward Blow

4. Grinding Palm

5. Expanding Fist

6. Single Lift and Punch

7. Raise and Strike with Arm

8. Rotate and Kneel

9. Disperse and Lock

10. Thrusting Palm Followed by
    a Double Kick with the Heel

Preview of Major Positions from the Ten Lines of Shao-Lin Chuan Tan-Tui

1

2

3

4

5

6

7

8

9

10

少林拳彈腿

Shao-Lin Chuan Tan-Tui
The Ten Lines of Springy-Legs

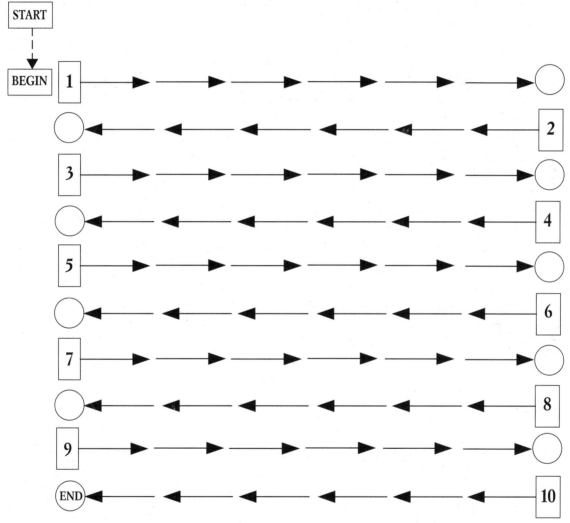

Each of the Ten Lines of Tan-Tui consists of a sequence of movements which is then performed in mirror image. (By convention, the original sequence is called the "right side" and the mirror image is called the "left side" of the line.) The student then repeats the movement sequences—right side, left side, right side, left side, etc.—as many times as space and/or stamina will allow.

Opening

Begin facing north (in practice the initial direction is a matter of choice; north will serve to establish a frame of reference for the following instructions). Put the feet together and stand straight (A). Then sink down into the following stance: The weight rests on the right foot, which is turned 45 degrees to the side, while the left foot sits forward, with only the ball touching the ground. Simultaneously bring both hands to the sides of the chest, palms up, thumbs bent, and fingers straight and slightly apart (B). Thrust both hands straight out in front with palms facing forward, crossing left hand over right hand (C). Put fingers together and swing both hands around to the back with the fingers curled back, pointing towards the elbows (D). Step forward with the left foot, then take two more steps and stop with feet together while both hands swing to the front of the chest, palms down (E). Make fists with both hands and turn them so the knuckles are facing up (F). Move fists together and form a cross by holding the left arm vertically behind the right arm with both fists facing inward (G). Punch the left fist upward while the right fist moves to the side of the chest with the knuckles facing up (H). This position (in this case, of the right fist) in which the fist (or open hand) is tucked under the armpit at the side will be referred to henceforth as a "chambered" fist. (The term "chambered" describes the tucked position of the fist or open palm, usually preceding a strike by the same hand or fist. The analogy is to a gun, in which the projectile is "chambered" before being fired.) Form a cross again by holding the right arm vertically behind the left arm (I). Then punch upward with the right fist. Simultaneously raise the left knee, turning the ankle so that the ball of the left foot is facing the right knee, toes pointed down. The left fist is placed just above the left thigh, near the knee, protecting the groin (J). This is called the golden post stance.

Opening

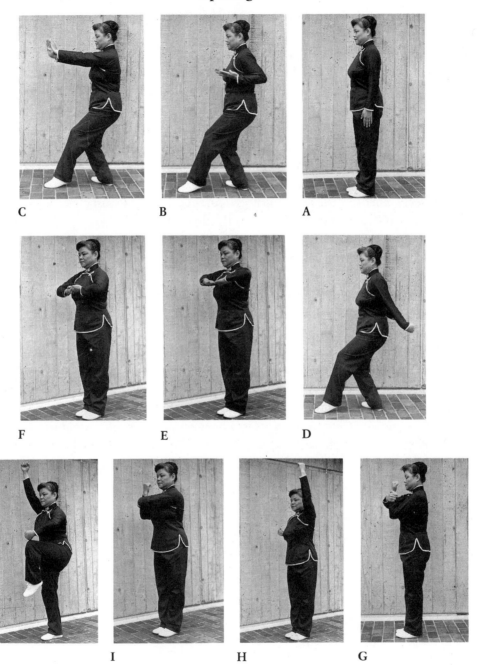

C   B   A

F   E   D

J   I   H   G

虎抱頭
1. Tiger Grasping the Head

Begin with the left fist up to the left side (A), while stepping to the left with the knee bent. The right leg is straight and the right arm and fist are trailing outstretched behind, parallel to the floor (B). Keep the body straight, look to the left side, and punch to the left (C). Turn the left toe in and bend the right knee, keeping the left leg straight and both feet parallel. At the same time, block up with the right fist, palm facing outward and the back of the hand near the temple. Block down and slightly forward with the left fist, placing it in front of the left knee with the back of the fist facing down (D). Rise from this position and pivot 75 degrees counterclockwise on the left foot, moving the right foot around. Bring both fists together and place below the chin, with knuckles facing the body (E). Then chamber the fists and punch to both sides simultaneously (F). Using the right fist, block to the waist (G). Bring the right toe to the arch of the left foot, stepping up (H). Kick straight toward the right, shoulder height, with the toe pointed (I). The right leg lands with the right knee bent, while the left leg is straight; this standard position of the legs (back leg straight, front leg bent, most of the weight shifted onto front leg) is called a bow-and-arrow stance. (The reader should understand that this term will be used frequently to describe this configuration of the lower body, regardless of what the upper body is doing.) Chamber the right fist while keeping the left arm and fist parallel to the floor, trailing behind (J). Punch with the right (K). Then lower the body, bending the left knee and straightening the right leg. The fists block in same manner described above, except in reverse: the left fist sits, palm out, near the left temple, while the right hand guards the right knee (L). Then shift 75 degrees clockwise, bringing the fists in front, back hand out, under the chin, and so on, a mirror image of the previous movement above (M–T). Repeat the entire exercise. End facing west in a bow-and-arrow stance, right knee forward, and right arm extended in a punch, with the left hand trailing behind parallel to the ground, hand forming a fist (K).

1. Tiger Grasping the Head

A　　　　　　　　B　　　　　　　　C

D　　　　　　　　E　　　　　　　　F

G　　　　　　　　H　　　　　　　　I

1. Tiger Grasping the Head

J

K

L

M

N

P

Q

R

S

T

歸車轉

2. Reverse Cartwheel

Bring the left foot forward next to the right, turning 90 degrees to face south. Extend the arms sideways, parallel to the ground and shoulder height, with hands forming fists (A). In a circular motion bring the right fist down, in, and up into a vertical position, elbow bent. The right fist (knuckles facing body) and forearm are inside of and perpendicular to the left fist and forearm, which have simultaneously circled over to form the horizontal axis of the now crossed forearms (B). This is the same crossed-arms position described previously (see I, p. 43), from which the golden post stance was formed. Again, form the golden post stance (see J, pg. 43), punching up with the right hand (C). Then chamber the right fist. Bend the left elbow, bringing the left forearm in front of the chest, with the left hand in front of the right shoulder, palm open and facing away from the body (D). Turning to the left, bring the left foot down on the left side to form a bow-and-arrow stance. The left knee should be bent and the right leg straight. At the same time, slap out with the open left hand, so that the palm faces out to the left (E). Pull the left hand back into chambered position, matching the right fist (F). Keeping the shoulders straight and stationary, punch forward with the right hand in a horizontal fist (G). Alternate punching with the right and left arms three more times (as one fist punches, the other extended fist is pulled back into a chambered position, and so on). This first series of punches is the only one with four—all the rest have only three. On the fourth punch, which is a left punch, kick the right leg up, next to the left fist, toes pointed (H). Let the right foot fall forward, bending the right knee, shifting the weight forward, and keeping the left (rear) leg straight—another bow-and-arrow stance (I). From that position, punch three times, ending with a right punch and a left leg kick, toes pointed, next to the right fist (J). Let the left foot fall forward, bending the left knee and straightening the right leg, again adopting a bow-and-arrow stance (K). The right fist should still be extended. Repeat, but finish with the left fist extended and right knee forward in a bow-and-arrow stance, facing east (I).

2. Reverse Cartwheel

D   C   B   A

G   F   E

K   J   I   H

2. Reverse Cartwheel

D   E   F

G   H   I

Positions shown from opposite camera angle.

劈 槃 槃

3. Strike With a Forward Blow

Bring the left foot up next to the right, turning 90 degrees to face north. Extend fists sideways as described above, and assume the golden post stance (A–C). Step to the left onto the left foot, bending the left knee and forming a bow-and-arrow stance, facing west. Simultaneously place the left fist at the left side of the chest, and extend the right fist and hand forward, fingers open (D). Punch with the left arm and simultaneously bring the right hand underneath the left armpit (rolling-sleeve-back position E). Then turn the left foot in so that both feet are parallel, shifting weight to the right, bending the right knee, and straightening the left leg. Simultaneously, making a fist with the right hand (the left hand is already a fist), swing both fists in an arc, down and then up, to the right side, shoulder-high. The left fist should be in front of the right shoulder (F). Keep looking to the left. Then swing the left arm and fist over like a hammer to the left side, striking with the back of the fist (G). Turn the body 75 degrees counterclockwise by bringing the right foot around behind, pivoting on the left leg; and form a "cross stance" by swinging the right fist over and down, while moving the left under and up (H). (The term "cross stance" refers to the fact that the outstretched fists form a sort of cross.) You should now have switched directions as a result of turning into the cross stance, with both arms outstretched sideways, hands forming fists. Look to the right (west). Block up with the left fist to the left temple, knuckles facing away from the body, and block down to the right waist with the right fist (I). Continue to look to the right side. Kick the right leg to the right with the toes pointed (J). Land with the right foot pointing west, right knee bent, to form a bow-and-arrow stance. Meanwhile, bring the right fist up from the waist into a chambered position. Simultaneously, extend the left arm forward, fingers open (K). Punch with the right fist and bring the left hand, palm open and fingers straight, underneath the right arm toward the right armpit (rolling-sleeve-back position L). Turn the right foot in so that both feet are parallel, and shift the body weight to the left side, bending the left knee and straightening the right leg. Swing both fists from below to the left side, shoulder-high. The right fist should be in front of the left shoulder (M). Look to the right (west). Using the right fist like a hammer, swing the right arm over in an arc from left to right (N). Turn the body 75 degrees to the right by bringing the right foot around behind, pivoting on the left leg, and swinging the arms and fists in the abovementioned manner, forming a cross stance, with both arms outstretched, hands held in fists, and head facing left, a mirror image of the earlier cross stance (O). Block, kick, and roll sleeve back (P–S). Repeat and finish facing west with the left fist and arm extended, in a bow-and-arrow stance (left knee forward and bent), and the right hand under the armpit (rolling-sleeve-back position S).

3. Strike With a Forward Blow

A

B

C

D

E

F

G

H

I

3. Strike With a Forward Blow

J   K   L

M   N   O

P   Q   R   S

撑 磨

4. Grinding Stone with Palm

Bring the right foot up alongside the left, turning to face south, extending fists sideways (A). Assume the golden post stance (B–C). Step to the left (east) with the left foot, bending the left knee and straightening the right leg. Extend the left arm straight with the palm up (thumb tucked in). Simultaneously chamber the right hand at the side, palm open and facing up (D). Step forward with the right foot into a bow-and-arrow stance (again this name refers only to the position of the body below the waist; the upper body's position may vary considerably),.and extend the right hand, palm up and fingers straight. Simultaneously, the left hand (open, palm up) slides beneath the right arm until it reaches a point just below the armpit (E). Bring the left foot behind the right foot. At the same time, bend the right arm, swinging the forearm around in front of the chest (open hand palm up), as the body turns 90 degrees counterclockwise. Turn the left hand palm down and place it under the right elbow. Look to the left (F). Chamber the right open hand and slap with the left hand leftward so that the elbow is straight, palm facing out (G). Turn the body a further 90 degrees counterclockwise and step back with the right foot, straightening the right (rear) leg (bow-and-arrow stance). At the same time, push straight forward with the right palm, and chamber the left fist (H). Bring the right hand to the right side of the chest, palm up and open, and open the left fist so that the palm is facing up also. Turn the body to the right so that it faces the opposite direction, bending the right knee and straightening the left leg. Extend the right arm straight forward over the right foot, palm up (I). Step forward with the left foot, forming a bow-and-arrow stance, and extend the left hand forward, palm up and fingers straight. At the same time, slide the right hand below the left arm to a point near the armpit, palm facing up (a mirror of the motion described above, see J). Bring the right foot behind the left foot, turning 90 degrees to the right. At the same time, swing the left forearm in front of the chest, keeping the palm up. Turn the right hand to a palm-down position and place under the left elbow, with the one forearm on top of the other (as above). Look to the right (K). Then separate the arms by chambering the open left hand, palm up, and slapping the right hand to the right so that the arm is straight and the palm faces out (L). Turn the body a further 90 degrees clockwise, and step back with the left foot to form a bow-and-arrow stance. At the same time, push straight forward with the left palm and chamber the right hand, forming a fist (M). Repeat entire movement. Always make sure that the thumbs are bent, and the torso is straight and not leaning forward. Finish in a bow-and-arrow stance, with the right hand extended and right leg forward, facing east (I).

4. Grinding Stone With Palm

C   B   A

F   E   D

H   G

4. Grinding Stone With Palm

K   J   I

M   L

4. Grinding Stone With Palm

I   J

K   L   M

Positions shown from opposite camera angle

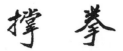

5. Expanding Fist

Bring the left foot up alongside the right, turning 90 degrees to face north. Assume the golden post stance (A–C). Turning 135 degrees to the left, step into a bow-and-arrow stance, shifting most of the weight onto the forward left foot (the body now faces southwest). Meanwhile, chamber the right fist, and simultaneously block up with the left fist, back of hand facing in, to the left temple (D). Punch forward with the right fist held vertically at shoulder-height (E). Then with the now-extended right fist, block down to the right waist (F). Kick the right foot forward with the toes pointed (G). Bring the right foot back to the instep of the left foot (H). Place the left fist at the left side of the chest, turn 90 degrees to the right, and punch with the right fist while darting forward, pushing off the left foot, stepping first with the right foot, and ending up with feet together and right fist extended (now facing northwest, I). Step forward with the left foot and swing up the right knee, while turning the toes of the right foot down over the left knee. Hold both fists, knuckles facing inward, in front of the chest, with the right fist higher than the left (J). Step forward with the right foot to form a bow-and-arrow stance, and block up with the right fist to the right temple, back of the hand facing in (knuckles facing away from the body). At the same time, punch forward with the left fist (K). Then block to the left waist with the left fist (L). Kick the left foot forward with the toes pointed (M). Bring the left foot to the instep of the right foot (N). Turn 90 degrees to the left and dart forward off the right foot, stepping first with the left foot, and ending up with feet together and the right fist at the right side of the chest, while punching straight forward (southwest) with the left fist (O). Step forward with the right foot and swing up the left knee, turning the left foot down over the right knee. Hold both fists (back of fists facing away from the body) in front of the chest, with the left fist higher than the right fist (P). Then step forward with the left foot to form a bow-and-arrow stance, and block up with the left fist to the temple. At the same time, punch forward with the right fist (Q). Repeat these movements, which zig-zag southwest and northwest, finishing in a bow-and-arrow stance, left leg forward and bent, right fist extended, facing southwest (E and Q).

5. Expanding Fist

A

B

C

D

E

F

G

H

I

5. Expanding Fist

J

K

L

M

N

O

P

Q

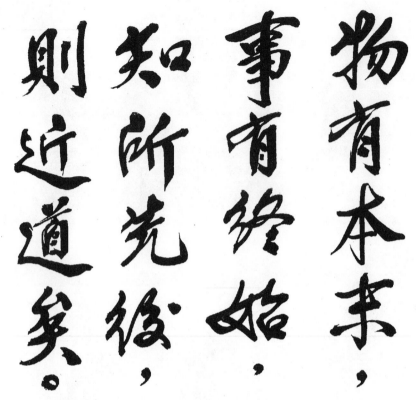

Things have their roots and branches, human affairs have their endings and beginnings, to know what comes first and what comes afterwards is to approach the principles of the great.
—Teaching of Confucius[6]

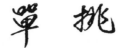

6. Single Lift and Punch

Bring the right leg up alongside the left, turning the body 45 degrees to face south and extending the fists sideways (A). Assume the golden post stance (B–C). Step to the left with the left foot to form a horse stance (both knees bent, weight in the middle), keeping the back straight and feet parallel. Hold the right fist just above shoulder level so that the arm forms a triangle, and place the left fist at the left side of the chest (D). Punch to the side with the left fist, while looking to the left (E). Lower the body, bending the right knee while straightening the left leg, and block down with the left fist to the left knee, back hand facing down (F). Open the left hand, and extend the left arm to the left toe in a horizontal slicing motion, with the palm down (G). Then bring the left hand to a chambered position at the left side of the chest, forming a fist, simultaneously rising up and forming a bow-and-arrow stance. At the same time, also chamber the right fist, adjusting the right leg a bit wider (to the right), then punch forward with the right fist (H). Block to the right waist with the right fist (I). Kick the right foot forward with toes pointed (J). After the right foot comes down from the kick, the left foot is placed behind the right foot, facing the opposite direction. Chamber both fists (K). Step to the right with the right foot to form a horse stance and bring the left fist back to just above the shoulder. Strike to the side with the right fist at shoulder level (L). Lower the body, bending the left knee and straightening the right leg, and block down with the right fist to the right knee (M). Open the right hand and extend the right arm to the right toe in a slicing motion, with palm down (N). Chamber the right hand, forming a fist, while rising to form a bow-and-arrow stance. Simultaneously chamber the left fist, adjusting the left leg a bit to the left, and punch forward with the left fist (O). Block to the left waist with the left fist (P). Kick the left foot forward with toes pointed (Q). After the left foot comes down from the kick, the right foot steps behind the left foot facing the opposite direction. Chamber both fists and look to the left (R). Step to the left with the left foot to form a horse stance and bring the right fist back to just above the shoulder, as the left fist punches to the left side (S). Repeat entire sequence. Finish in a horse stance, chest facing north, left fist cocked near left temple, and right fist extended to right side, with head looking to the right, in direction of just-released punch (L).

6. Single Lift and Punch

D   C   B   A

G   F   E

J   I   H

6. Single Lift and Punch

M   L   K

P   O   N

S   R   Q

Students can now begin to practice this stretch (shown above) and sitting down exercise (below) in preparation for Line 8.

挑 打

7. Raise and Strike

Bring left foot next to right, turning head to face north (the rest of the body should already be oriented in this direction) and extending fists sideways (A). Assume the golden post stance (B–C). Step to the left with the left foot to form a horse stance. Simultaneously bring the right fist back above the right shoulder and chamber the left fist, punching to the left with the left fist at shoulder level from the horse stance (D). Lower the body, bending the right knee while straightening the left leg, moving the right fist slightly up next to the right temple. Drop the extended left arm and fist next to the left toe (E). Then turn the body to face west and rise, swinging the left fist up in front of the left ear in a guard position and chambering the right fist (F). Kick the right foot forward with the toes pointed, keeping the arms in the same position (G). Step forward with the right foot, bringing the left foot next to the arch of the right foot. At the same time, drop the left fist from the guard position to the side of the chest, chambering it, and punch in the direction of the step (H). Turning 90 degrees, sidestep to the left with the left foot, and bring the right foot next to the left foot's arch. Simultaneously punch leftward (sideways) with the left fist, while also looking to the left (I–J). Bring the right forearm forward into a vertical position with the fist at eye level (palm facing body) and place the left wrist under the elbow, opening the left hand and bending the wrist so that the fingers point up, with the right elbow resting within the resulting hollow formed by the horizontal left forearm and upturned hand (K). Move the left hand up past the right hand to above the left shoulder, forming a fist (L). At the same time, bring the right fist down the side of the chest, chambering it, and side-step to the right with the right foot, bringing the left toe up next to the right arch and punching sideways to the right with the right fist (M). Step to the left with the left foot, forming a horse stance with both feet parallel. Lower the body, bending the left knee and straightening the right leg, raising the left fist above the shoulder to near the left temple. Drop the extended right arm and fist next to the right toe (N). Swing the right fist up in front of the right ear and bring the left fist to the left side of the chest, chambering it (as above, except that you have switched sides) while turning the body and right toe to face west again in bow-and-arrow stance (O). Kick the left foot forward with the toes pointed, keeping the arms in the same position (P). Step forward with the left foot, bringing the right foot forward and placing it next to the arch of the left foot. At the same time, chamber then punch the right fist in the direction of the step (Q). Turn 90 degrees to the right, side-step to the right, and bring the left toe next to the arch of the right foot, allowing the left foot to rest there on its ball. Punch with the right fist sideways to the right while looking to the right (R–S). Bring the left forearm in front held vertically at eye level and place the right wrist under the elbow, opening the right hand in the manner described above (T). Then move the right hand up in front past the left hand and, forming a fist, bring it to the right side, above the shoulder and near the temple (U).

At the same time, chamber the left fist and sidestep to the left with the left foot, bringing the right toe up next to the left arch and punching sideways to the left with the left fist (V). Repeat entire set of movements. Finish with a right-handed side-punch and the chest facing south (M).

7. Raise and Strike

A

B

C

D

E

F

G

H

7. Raise and Strike

I J K

L M N

O P Q

7. Raise and Strike

R

S

T

U

V

軺環蹲

8. Rotate and Kneel

Face south, bring feet together, and stand with fists extended sideways (A). Assume the golden post stance (B–C). Step to the left with the left foot to form a horse stance. Bring the right fist back near the temple (or above the right shoulder) and the left fist to the side of the chest (D). Punch to the left side with the left fist (E). Lower the body, bending the right knee and straightening the left leg. Keep the right fist at the temple and block down with the left fist in front of the left knee (F). Rise up, form a bow-and-arrow stance, and bring both fists, palms toward body, under the chin in front of the chest (G). Chamber both fists at sides and punch out sideways (H). This is the cross stance. Block to the center line with the right fist so that the right forearm is held vertically, palm toward body (I). Kick up with the right heel (J). As the right leg descends from its kick, bring the right foot forward to form a bow-and-arrow stance, chamber the right fist at the side, and punch. Meanwhile, the left hand should trail behind, straight back, parallel to the ground, at shoulder height (K–L). Lower the body, bending the left leg and straightening the right leg. Block up with the left hand and down with the right (M). Rise up to form a bow-and-arrow stance, adjusting the left (rear) foot a bit to the side to give the stance its proper width (as usual) and placing fists under the chin in front of the chest, palms in (N). Chamber fists at sides and punch sideways (O). Block to the center line with the left fist, so that the left forearm is held vertically, palm toward body (P). Kick up with the left heel (Q). Keeping the left leg in the air at waist level, spin to the right 270 degrees, simultaneously chambering both fists (R). Landing with the left leg over the right leg, lower the body into the Buddha Sitting position. The left foot is flat and the right heel is off the ground (S). Look to the right and punch to the left side with the left fist (T). Rise up from the Buddha Sitting position on left leg (U), and kick to the right with the right heel as the body becomes upright (V). Let the right leg land forward and shift weight forward into the bow-and-arrow stance. Punch with the right fist in the direction you are looking, leaving the left arm extended behind (W). Lower the body, bending the left knee and straightening the right leg. Bring the left fist next to left temple and block down with the right fist in front of right knee (X). Rise and form a bow-and-arrow stance (bending right knee and shifting weight forward), adjust the rear leg, and bring both fists, palm in, under the chin in front of the chest (Y). Chamber both fists and punch sideways (Z). Block with the left fist to the center line so that the left forearm is held vertically, palm facing in (AA). Kick up with the left heel (BB). Allow the left foot to land forward and shift the weight forward into a bow-and-arrow stance while chambering the left fist. Punch forward with the left fist. The right fist should trail straight back, arm parallel to the ground. Look to the left (CC). Lower the body, bending the right knee and straightening the left leg. Bring the right fist to the temple, and block down with the left fist in front of the knee (DD). Rise up to form a bow-and-arrow stance and place fists under the chin in front of the chest, palms facing in (EE). Chamber the fists at the sides and punch sideways (FF). Block to the center line with the right fist, so that the right forearm is held vertically, palm toward the body (GG). Kick up with the right heel (HH). Keeping the right leg in the air at waist level, spin to the left 270 degrees, bringing both fists into a chambered position (II). Landing with the right leg over the left leg, lower the body into the Buddha Sitting position. The right foot is flat and the left heel is off the ground (JJ). Look to the left and punch to the right side with the right fist (KK). Rise up from the Buddha Sitting position on the right leg (LL), and kick up and to the side with the left heel after the body becomes fully upright (MM). Allow the left leg to land forward and shift weight forward into the bow-and-arrow stance (NN). Then punch forward at shoulder height with the left fist and keep the right arm and fist extended behind at shoulder-height (OO). Repeat entire sequence. Finish in a bow-and-arrow stance (right knee forward), facing east, with the right fist extended (having just punched), and the left arm and fist trailing behind parallel to the ground (L).

8. Rotate and Kneel

C   B   A

F   E   D

I   H   G

8. Rotate and Kneel

L   K   J

O   N   M

R   Q   P

8. Rotate and Kneel

U

T

S

X

W

V

AA

Z

Y

8. Rotate and Kneel

DD

CC

BB

GG

FF

EE

JJ

II

HH

8. Rotate and Kneel

MM

LL

KK

OO

NN

碰 销

9. Disperse and Lock

Bring the left foot up alongside the right, turning 90 degrees to face north and extending the fists sideways (A). Assume the golden post stance (B–C). Step to the left with the left foot, turning the body 90 degrees to face west, and adopt a bow-and-arrow stance. Simultaneously, raise the left hand high above the head to join the right (D), then swing the arms down, first the right and then the left, so that the hands open and stop just above the bent left knee, left hand on top (E). Then swing hands together back up and over head, pulling the arms straight back behind the body and bringing the fingers together, pointed up toward elbows (F). Kick forward with the right foot, toes pointed (G). Step forward with the right foot to form a bow-and-arrow stance and swing both hands up over the head with the right hand on top of the left hand (H). Swing arms down to just above the right knee, with the right hand on top (as above, except with hands reversed, I). Swing hands back up and over the head (as above), pulling the arms straight back behind the body and bringing the fingers together, pointed up toward elbows (J). Kick the left leg up, toes pointed (K). Repeat (L–M). Finish with the right knee forward, hands just above it, chest and head facing west (I).

9. Disperse and Lock

A

B

C

D

E

F

G

H

I

9. Disperse and Lock

J

K

L

M

掌撑蹬撑

10. Thrusting Palm Followed by a Double Kick with the Heel

Bring the left foot up alongside the right, turning 90 degrees to face south. Stand up with the feet together and the arms outstretched to the sides (A). Assume the golden post stance (B–C). Step to the left side with the left foot to form a horse stance. Place the back of the right fist above the right shoulder and the left fist at the side of the chest (chambered). Look to the left (D). Punch to the left with the left fist at shoulder level (E). Bring the left leg back in and up so that the knee is raised and the toe pointed down toward the left. This is called the one-leg-standing position (the cock-stands-on-one-leg), quite similar to the position of the legs in the golden post stance. At the same time, open the left fist and swing the left hand in a circular motion, palm open and facing down, past the left knee (F), pausing with the hand in front of the face (G). Turning the body to the left, step forward with the left foot and swing the left hand forward in a hooking motion, allowing it to continue down; using the left foot as a pivot, bring the right foot 180 degrees counterclockwise so that both feet are parallel. Without pausing, lower the body, bending the left knee and straightening the right leg. The left arm has kept swinging behind and is now held straight behind the body, with the fingers together and pointed up toward the elbow. The right arm (which follows the left in a windmill-like motion) is now extended next to the right foot, hand open and palm facing away from the foot. Look to the right (H). Rise up to a bow-and-arrow stance and adjust the left leg to the left slightly, widening the stance for better balance, keeping the left arm and hand behind the left side in the same position. Move the right palm back to the side of the chest, chambering the open hand (I). Push the right palm forward (J), and then chamber it again, palm up, at the side of the chest (K). At the same time, lift the left foot up with the knee in front of the chest to prepare for a "double kick" (L). Kick slightly with the left foot, and then drive the left leg down while kicking up with the right heel (M). Step forward with the right foot to form a bow-and-arrow stance and thrust forward with the right palm (N). Turn the body 90 degrees to the left, bringing the right leg in and up, raising the knee, into the one-leg-standing position. At the same time swing the right hand in a circular motion, palm open and facing down, past the right knee (O), pausing in front of the face (P). Step forward with the right foot and use it as a pivot; swinging the right hand forward in a hooking motion, allow it to continue down and back, using its momentum (and the pivotal right leg) to swing around the left leg 180 desgrees clockwise so that the feet are parallel and more than a shoulder width apart. Without pausing, lower the body, bending the right knee and straightening the left leg. The right arm has completed its swing back and is now held behind the body, with the fingers together and pointed up toward the elbow. The left arm (which follows the right in a windmill-like motion) is now extended next to the left foot, palm open and facing out. Look to the left (Q). Rise up to a bow-and-arrow stance and slightly adjust the right leg to the right for better balance. Move the left hand palm up to the side of the chest, into a chambered position (R). Push the left palm forward. Then chamber the open left hand again. Lift the right foot up in front of the chest to prepare for a double kick (S). Kick slightly with the right leg, and then drive the right foot straight down, while kicking up with the left heel (T). Step forward with the left foot as it is landing after the kick, form a bow-and-arrow stance, and push forward with the left palm (U). Repeat. Finish in a bow-and-arrow stance, right leg forward, right palm thrust forward, facing east (J).

10. Thrusting Palm Followed by a Double Kick with the Heel

B

A

D

C

G

F

E

10. Thrusting Palm Followed by a Double Kick with the Heel

J   I   H

M   L   K

P   O   N

10. Thrusting Palm Followed by a Double Kick with the Heel

S   R   Q

U   T

Closing

Bring the left foot up alongside the right, turning the body 90 degrees, and stand facing north, extending the fists sideways (A). Assume the golden post stance (B–C). Then with the right fist make a big circle downward (clockwise), letting the fist pause in front of the raised left knee (D). Step to the left with the left foot to form a horse stance. Simultaneously bring the right fist (palm facing away from the body) above the right shoulder, driving the right elbow sideways, and chamber the left fist (E), immediately punching to the left with the left fist at shoulder height (F). Be sure you are looking in the direction of the punch (left). Bring the left foot next to the right foot, legs straight and together. Bring downward-facing fists, knuckles together, in front of body, elbows at shoulder height (G). Return both fists to the sides of the body and open palms (H). This completes the Ten Lines of Shao-Lin Chuan Tan-Tui.

Closing

A

B

C

D

E

F

G

H

Method

In performing Shao-Lin Chuan Tan-Tui, the challenge is to maintain a relaxed yet straight posture of the torso, neck, and head while executing a well-timed and well-coordinated series of kicks, punches, blocks, leaps, crouches, and turns. Being mindful of the posture of the upper body allows the core energy of the body to flow freely into and out of the central nervous system. Any unnecessary tension, whether a clenched jaw or a restricted diaphragm, affects the entire body.

The smooth carriage of the torso involves engaging only those muscles that are necessary to perform a particular movement. Muscles occur and are activated in groups. For example, when kicking, the leg muscles are active, with the pelvis and spine forming the fulcrum. The muscle groups of the upper body are not activated, except for the muscles involved in respiration.

Because the Tan-Tui set is rigorous, old patterns of unnecessary tension often arise in the course of practice. With the assistance of the teacher, new and more effective methods of breathing and using muscles can be developed. A common tendency is to tense the face and hold the breath just before performing a difficult kick or spin. This is the opposite of the general relaxation and smooth breathing needed to perform the movements successfully. This same principle applies to the eyes, whose gaze should be unwavering.

Timing is crucial. Since each of the ten lines consists of a set of movements that is performed repeatedly, it is essential to find a smooth pace. The rhythm of outer movement is related to the rhythm of breathing, which becomes progressively deeper and smoother with practice. Pacing is an individual matter determined by the capacities and limitations of one's strength and stamina. Finding a suitable rhythm is an ongoing process. What feels like the optimum pace may change over time. In any case, one should avoid rushing the movement to the point where breathing becomes labored and movements uncoordinated. Pausing a few moments between lines may be helpful to regain composure.

Another aspect of timing is related to the coordination of the movement. Each of the kicks and punches needs to be executed so that the dynamic force of the body emanates from the center. This force is focused and expressed down from the waist and legs into the earth and up through the torso and arms, and out of the hands. In this way, any shift in the body's momentum is utilized to augment and focus the force of each movement.

Voluntary relaxation of different muscle groups is required for well-coordinated and balanced movement. A common hindrance to such relaxation is the chronic tension so common in modern society. In particular, it is difficult to relax muscles deep within the abdomen and pelvis, although these muscles are essential for upright posture and optimum breathing. Relaxation of the diaphragm and other muscles involved in respiration can be achieved gradually through the aware-ness of breathing, or *chi*. Breathing is the result of muscle contractions, as are all movements, but its uniqueness lies in being a partly voluntary, partly involuntary function. Up to a point, it is possible to control the depth and pace of breathing. Through awareness it is possible to slowly deepen and expand breathing so that the entire body begins to relax.

The "spiritual" (non-physical) aspect of relaxation has to do with a clear awareness of oneself, and an understanding of one's motivation for practicing. A practice that is based in fear, anger, or divisive ambition ultimately becomes tense and bears bitter fruit. It is the responsibility of the martial arts teacher to witness and reflect upon the non-physical aspects of the student's practice. The teacher can then help guide the student toward a harmonious relationship to his/her practice and personal life.

Chinese Philosophy and Religion
Related to Shao-Lin Chuan

Since martial arts practice is directed toward both outer and inner development, it is not surprising that martial arts teachers draw upon the rich heritage of Chinese philosophy and religion in order to guide and encourage their students. A traditional and complete approach to training in the martial arts includes physical, mental, and spiritual development and discipline. The goal is a harmonious balance, both within the individual and in his/her relationship to the world.

In the process of training, students discover and develop new skills. They also inevitably encounter deeply entrenched limitations, both personal and generically human. It is the teacher's responsibility to mirror and accompany the student through the enthusiasm and frustration that arise in the process. While students generally gain stability and emotional strength through martial arts training, along the way they may experience emotional upheaval and periods of anger, grief, boredom, and despair. With perseverance these frustrations will give way to periods of peak interest, satisfaction, and delight.

At difficult points, students can be encouraged from the wisdom of the "three ways" of Chinese culture: Taoism, Confucianism, and Buddhism.

From the Taoist tradition, the student may be encouraged to simplify his/her approach to movement and to life as a whole. It is essential to keep coming back to the basics of focusing on the body and discovering its real needs: proper nutrition, rest, exercise, and companionship. In the complex, artificial, and at times overstimulating environments of the modern world, such basic knowledge about the human body is often ignored. Taoism teaches the importance of harmonious enjoyment of the natural world, beginning with one's own body. While training movements may appear forceful, the student must always seek to remain centered and relaxed. A skillful approach to martial arts movement involves the practice of *wu wei*, or effortless action, and the related Taoist idea of flowing like water, without resistance.

From Confucianism, the student may be encouraged to cultivate an attitude of respect, not without severity, but tempered by tolerance. Such an attitude begins with oneself, then extends into the student's relationships with others. The Confucian principle that all human beings deserve to be treated as living subjects and not as objects is important in this regard. The teacher/student relationship should function as a model for balanced and satisfying relationships. The Confucian emphasis on respect for the ancestors and hierarchy in relationships is an important aspect of the teacher/student relationship, as the teacher occupies the role of elder.

Finally, Buddhism provides for the wise use of energies that arise in the course of martial arts practice. With its doctrines of nonviolence (harmlessness) and correct livelihood, Buddhism helps to temper the anger and arrogance that may arise during the student's practice. Buddhism emphasizes the direct experience of consciousness, which grows out of bodily balance and awareness into a heightened experience of compassion and wisdom. These attributes equip the student to meet difficulties that arise in the course of martial arts practice with dignity and understanding.

A man should not worry that other people do not recognize his merits, he should only worry that he has failed to recognize the merits of other people.
—Confucius[7]

Yu Chou Chuang
Universal Stance/Post of Life

The Universal Stance helps you gather strength through the development of mental concentration in a motionless exercise. This exercise requires you to stand upright and not lean towards one side or the other. Support yourself on one leg without tightening your muscles or bending that leg. Put the other leg forward and let it serve as a point of balance. Raise your arms forward and spread them to form a ring at shoulder height, as if you were embracing someone. (If the right foot is forward, the right hand is out a little bit farther than the left; see picture p. 95. If the left foot is forward, the left hand is out farther). Breathe freely and naturally; look forward. Imagine that you are standing on a high mountaintop overlooking the ocean, and let your mental vision concentrate on looking out across the water toward the horizon. Then, allow all the muscles throughout your body to relax (which also permits the blood to flow freely) so that you feel the *chi* sinking to the *tan-tien* (an energy center within the lower abdomen, just below the navel). Stop whenever you begin to feel strain in your arms or tension in your shoulders. Do not force yourself beyond what feels good.

The aim of this exercise is to gather strength without making a physical effort, by concentrating all thought on activating the *chi*, which nourishes strength. Thus, the main emphasis is on the development of the will. This outwardly motionless exercise requires no physical exertion and needs no muscular development. When you do this exercise, you must concentrate and think only about what you are doing. Performed in this manner, the Universal Stance renews your energy and vitality.

For the cultivation of mental health, an effort should be made to achieve peace of mind while doing this silent exercise. Success comes from the relaxation of the body, the relaxation of the mind, the relaxation of the *chi*, and the freedom of the soul. Mental strength is the core of this exercise. Eventually, you feel that the whole universe is at your fingertips and that you are standing in the center of the world.

Therefore, the Universal Stance provides you with an opportunity to develop concentration, patience, and perseverance, but success will come only over a long period of time. Do not be impatient; never give up halfway through. Do the exercise every morning in the early hours (before sunrise) when the air is freshest. With sincere effort and practice, with diligence and determination, you will ultimately reap great physical, mental, and spiritual benefits.

健身之道

Way to Health[8]

宇宙椿

Internal System (Exercise)
Yu Chou Chuang, Universal Stance

拳無拳
意無意
無意之中是真意
道真竅不真
修道往勞身

Fist, and yet, not a fist.
Meaning, and yet, no meaning;
Within the midst of meaninglessness is the true meaning.
To speak of truth is to be intelligent of no truth;
To cultivate the Way is to leave the body of toil.[9]

郭 師 父 連 蔭

The Universal Stance was Sifu's favorite exercise;
he always encouraged students to do it correctly.[10]

宇宙樁（不動的運動）
Yu Chou Chuang, Universal Stance or The Post of Life

姿勢必須站正，全身不倚不偏，表現均衡，重心常在垂直線上，雙腳虛實分明，兩手成環抱狀，呼吸聽其自然合乎宇宙的節拍，絲毫不得做作，頭往上頂，有頂意而不用力，騁目舒懷，全身關節渾元，而無稜角，肘腿似直非直似曲非曲，任其自然，筋絡伸展，渾身放鬆，不稍有淤滯之處，氣自下沉，而歸丹田，兩膝意識上往上縱，兩內腳跟往外撐，毛髮直翌，週身發射光芒．

此為定勁工夫，以在靜中得勁為準，純以聚神於身，以神御氣，以氣生勁，故以精神與意志為最重要，這種不在苦體勞珍，外表「不動的運動」，不費氣力，無需發達肌肉，而能影響到大肌肉內部的微血管層．

在單純中求其變化，於形態上表現生氣磅薄，有一種很自然的雄偉氣魄，從任何角度來看，都是科學的，凝重而不呆板，充分具備了體能的美，不僅是一種健身藝術，而且是一種怡情養性的靜默工夫，可培養毅力，從世俗的煩亂中獲得舒暢，在現實中求超現實的寄託，具有極高的精神價值，要促成一切意象具體化，豐富的想象具體化，豐富的想象力是必要的條件，從單純而莊嚴的形象中見出無窮，於有限中發現無限．

努力保持內心的平靜，不要著象成為澄澈真空，身鬆則輕，心鬆則靜，氣鬆則鼓蕩，神聞則氣安，是第一等工夫，在種種修練中，以練心為最難，而心力之強也是無堅不摧，在寧靜安息中深遠，使心物趨於一元，才能達到透明的地步，不受任何拘束，舒適而流暢，舒展快樂的幻想，整個的宇宙都是你的，立足點正是世界的中心，一片空曠而沒有任何畛域，如在無人之境，兩眼遠視如對蒼天碧海，把雄視宇宙的精神表現出來，兩耳像在靜聽世界的號叫，把自己放大，似欲將整個宇宙秉撐破，日久自有超俗的強烈感覺，予人一種穩定感，如同我們郭老師連蔭公站樁時，使人看後會產生強烈雄偉，氣勢逼人的感覺．

　　站樁時，注意力集中，置全念於撐與抱之意識上，基於心無二用的道理，其他一切散亂的思慮不復存在，就能使你的心懷一片空靈，如此往復練習，漸入自我催眠之階段，且由於這種心理的影響，對於細胞組織和身體的機能都具有刺激的作用，在身心兩方面獲得無窮的好處，產生運行不息之意志力量，從而控制與利用之，此項會心妙悟之功力，即為神秘生命力之泉源．

　　機會是永恆的，若有堅定信念，忍耐與毅力，以創造代替折磨，在自強不息中，細水長流，日久天長，方收練習之效，切忌躁急，力戒近效，應作為日常起居之一部份，不要半途而廢，每晨無間風雨，嚴肅認真練習，每日以早晨為宜，因黎明的空氣清新，而這種工夫的姿勢，可使呼吸深入，可增單位時間所吸入新鮮的氧氣量，可以澄清血液中廢物，血脈暢通無阻，可驅散憂鬱，可防止及治癒體內生理上所起之一切障礙，強肝強腎，精神振奮飽滿，可以防止本未老先衰及避免種種心臟病，且能幫助心臟肌肉內的血液循環，強壯的心臟是快樂長壽的條件，使你享受一個從精神上發揮出來的更長久，更豐富和更光輝的人生，它能產生一種沛然難禦的驚人潛力，這種十倍於天性的潛力，將隨著時間發展，而至無可抗拒，此為在他人之間，已成為事實之事，在吾人之間，當亦可能實現，吾人應抱定堅強之信心，努力練習，因「一種自信有把握或確信的態度，本身就可影響其後果．」這是一種求己的工夫，權操在己，有求必應，不為天賦所限，可由學習而得，至各人智慧悟力及稟賦不同，僅係過渡時期之長短而已，只須勤慎努力，終必有所成就．

Extensive Study, Constant Practice.
—*Confucius*[11]

I consider it a blessing to study with Simu, who embodies both the form and spirit of the Chinese martial arts. Learning to teach is a great challenge in learning to apply the principles creatively so that others may benefit as well.
— *Jeffrey Kessler*

Teacher's individual attention helps enthusiastic blind student to learn, SFSU.

Lin Hsueh-Chin

林雪琴

San Francisco State University lecture class on Chinese philosophy and martial arts.

The following two essays were written by my faithful student Dan Wang for independent study at SFSU. They indicate in Chinese style some directions for future study and research.

原始自然繼現代科學

Sources of Tai-Chi Philosophy and Modern Science

Dan Wang

The Tai-Chi system originated with Fu-Hsi (2953–2838 B.C.E.). Born in Shan-Si Province, he was first of the Five Emperors of the legendary period of China. At first, the term Tai-Chi was a label for the sun, and Yin and Yang were used to designate the shady and sunny sides of a building or a tree. Tai-Chi is rooted in oneness and the complementary interplay of two polar forces: Yin and Yang. By using the symbols (━ ━) and (━━━) to represent these two forces, respectively, the Eight Trigrams[12]—the key feature of the Tai-Chi system—were developed. The following chart illustrates the trigrams.[13]

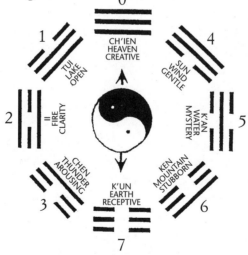

Note

The trigrams are arranged in opposite pairs having opposite symbologies such as heaven across from earth, fire from water, and so forth.

They are arranged in terms of opposite mathematics—each is obtained from its opposite by replacing broken lines with solid lines; also $2^3 = 8$ (Eight Trigrams).

The concept of the eight trigrams was further extended by subsequent generations of scholars (such as Lao-Tzu, Chuang-Chou, Chou Tun-I, Chu-Hsi, etc.) into sixty-four hexagrams[14] of the Tai-Chi system in the book of *I-Ching.* The hexagrams incorporate primal polarities on many levels, such as activity-stillness, day-night, light-dark, male-female, hot-cold, odd-even, and positive-negative.

This duality presupposes a unitive principle that is the source and support of the opposites emerging from it. Without the experience of unity, the opposites conflict and diverge. With the experience of unity, the opposites make up the inherent harmony, free from conflict and error, which in turn creates the trinity: Yin and Yang complement and balance each other in the Oneness. That is the Tao, the Way. The interaction of the affirming, denying, and harmonizing forces is integrated in all phenomena. This threefold unity of forces has long been a central feature of ancient Chinese philosophy and the wisdom teachings. The extraordinary and enduring popularity of the Tai-Chi system in the book of *I-Ching* is due in part to the fact that it presents a way in which the Tao, through the dual forces and the threefold fusion, can be related to the manifold forms of life, to the ten thousand creatures, and to the ethical and social decisions we confront daily.

Today we can see that the Tai-Chi system in the book of *I-Ching* is not only a binary system relevant to the development of computer science in our time, but also a cosmological and philosophical system based upon the same principles as the new "scientific" cosmology, principles of relativity and quantum physics, and higher mathematics. That is why the *I-Ching,* which can be traced back more than five thousand years, is still very much alive even to this day all over the world. Even today, in the Western world alone, there are new translations, and explanations, and brand-new versions of *I-Ching* by different authors appearing at the rate of several volumes each year.

First of all, the Tai-Chi system is based on the binary numbers, which is a two-value system (電腦二進位), like "ON" or "OFF" circuitry. The Yin line corresponds to the open circuit, or "OFF" position, because it is open in the middle of the line (━━ ━━). The Yang line corresponds the closed circuit, or "ON" position, because its center is closed (━━━━). If we substitute the Yin line with number zero (0) and the Yang line with number one (1), as Leibnitz did in the seventeenth century, we begin to see the implications of hexagrams to the binary system. Was Mr. Leibnitz' discovery of binary arithmetic independent of hexagrams? Whatever the relationship between Leibnitz' work and the natural arrangement of hexagrams, it is reasonable to believe that the usefulness of the binary system was not known in Western culture until the time of Leibnitz. Martin Gardner says: "It was not until the time of Leibnitz that the Fu-Hsi sequence was recognized as being isomorphic with a useful arithmetical notation."[15]

So, in addition to its popular uses in China, the Tai-Chi system of *I-Ching* also provided the basic patterns for the development of computer technology.

Leibnitz also wrote: "Everybody believes that Fu-Hsi was one of the old Emperors of China, one of the best known philosophers of the world, and at the same time the founder of scholarship in the Chinese Empire and in the Far East. His I-Ching table, handed down to the world, is the oldest monument of scholarship."[16] In this respect, Fu-Hsi, to whom the natural order of hexagrams is attributed, deserves the credit and praise.

Secondly, in addition to the useful binary system of the *I-Ching,* the cosmology (歐美天文學) the structural aspects of cosmic process) that the *I-Ching* presupposes is far more relevant to the natural origin of the universe than that of the classical Western tradition of cosmological science before the twentieth century, when Western cosmology was characterized by purely materialistic, mechanistic, and deterministic outlooks. Things were thought to move in time and space according to a predetermined or definite order. Space and time were regarded as independent elements. The world was viewed as a machine that followed the law of cause and effect. This idea was clearly expressed in the traditional three-dimensional space of Euclidean geometry, which prevailed until the beginning of the twentieth century; even Newtonian physics did not make any radical break with this kind of static cosmology. Such a worldview is certainly strange to the worldview of *I-Ching.*

However, that traditional view which held for many centuries was altered by development of modern science in the twentieth century. The new worldview, which is primarily attributed to Albert Einstein (1879–1955), is based on the theory of relativity and quantum mechanics. It is amazingly similar to the organic view of the world that the *I-Ching* suggests. This "new" organic worldview denies any absolute space and time categorization. Time and space become the dimensions of existence, and they are interdependent—nothing is isolated from the whole. Everything is related to everything else as if all were part of one organism. This organic view of the world can be seen in the ideas of Darwin, Freud, and Einstein, who got away from the dominant mechanistic view.

Such changes in Western scientific thought were strongly stimulated, if not indeed derived, from the organic world-outlook that is characteristically Chinese. The basic principle of the changing process in the *I-Ching* presupposes the organic view of the world. In other words, change is always accompanied by procreativity, which is the essential quality of any organism.

Likewise, the interaction of Yin and Yang presupposes their offspring—a creative process. Therefore, in a later period, this idea became important in the development of organic naturalism by many scholars like Chuang-Chou, Chou Tun-I, Chu-Hsi, etc. One of the leading Western scholars of Eastern thought, Joseph Needham, sums up the importance of the organic view of Chinese philosophy to the development of contemporary science as follows:

> *The time was to come when the growth of knowledge necessitated the adoption of a more organic philosophy no less naturalistic than atomic materialism. That was the time of Darwin, Frazer, Pasteur, Freud, Spemann, Planck, and Einstein. When it came, a line of philosophical thinkers was found to have prepared the way—from Whitehead back to Engels and Hegel, from Hegel to Leibnitz—then perhaps the inspiration was not European at all. Perhaps the theoretical foundations of the most modern European natural science owes more to the men such as Chuang-Chou, Chou Tun-I, and Chu-Hsi than the world has yet realized.*[17]

Since the rise of organic philosophy was largely based on the cosmology of the Tai-Chi system of *I-Ching,* the *I-Ching* can be regarded as the foundation of the most modern view of the world. It is based on the idea that the world is constantly in the process of change and transformation. The world changes because the essence of the world is none other than change itself, according to the *I-Ching.* The dynamic process of change and transformation is clearly expressed within the study of astronomic science as well as the study of quantum mechanics. The galaxies recede from one another, and new ones are formed by condensation out of the newly created matter. Old galaxies disappear, and new ones are formed.

Furthermore, the ever-moving orbital electrons and nucleus of subatomic structure seem to confirm the world of constant transformation. The world is relative because it is ongoing and constantly changing.

Thirdly, along with the value of the binary number system and new cosmology, Einstein's Theory of Relativity (愛因斯坦) supports the changing worldview. It denies that the world is static and absolute. Time and space are not independent—they are mutually complementary. The Theory of Relativity acknowledges that frames of reference are relative, and that one is as good as another. All motions are relative. In the world of relativity we cannot speak of anything objectively without making reference to its relationship with other things. This idea is central to the Yin and Yang relationship in the *I-Ching.* Yin is always relative to Yang, and Yang is always relative to Yin. Yin loses its meaning when its relationship with Yang is lost. Also, Yang is Yang because of Yin. The significance of the Yin and Yang relationship is clearly expressed in Einstein's special Theory of Relativity.

Let us take a good look at the mass-energy equivalence formula: $E=mc^2$. "E" signifies energy that is contained in a stationary body; "m" is its mass; and "c" is the velocity of light, about 186,000 miles per second. The energy that belongs to the mass is equal to this mass multiplied by the square of the enormous speed of light. This means that a vast amount of energy is needed for every unit of mass. The importance is the interdependence between energy and mass. Since c^2 is a constant, c^2 is a conditional factor. When the c^2 is provided, mass can become energy and energy can become mass. They are interchangeable when the c^2 is provided. Therefore, E or energy is always relative to mass, just as mass is relative to energy. In other words, energy cannot exist without mass, and mass cannot exist without energy. This is practically identical with the Yin and Yang relationship. The theory of relativity denies not only any absolute category of description but also the mechanical and deterministic view of the world.

However, even more important than the binary system, relativity and quantum physics, and cosmology is the Principle of Complementarity (相輔相成) of the opposites that both the *I-Ching* and modern science share.

According to *I-Ching,* everything consists of Yin and Yang, which are the basic constituents of all things. When there is Yin, there must be Yang. One does not exist without its counterpart. This idea seems to be realized in quantum mechanics as well. The discovery of the anti-electron and "antimatter" is certainly an important event, which coincides with Yin and Yang theory. When there is strong, there must be weak. When there is good, there must be evil. Just as Yin presupposes the existence of Yang, and vice versa, matter presupposes the existence of its counterpart, the antimatter. Even though these counterparts are exclusive because of their opposite character, they are complementary. Since they are subordinated to the wholeness to which they belong, they do not conflict with each other. In the field of quantum mechanics, these phenomena are called the "Principle of Complementarity," which was discovered by Danish physicist Niels Bohr during his study of light. That Principle of Complementarity is recognized and accepted as a crucial factor in the interpretation of quantum theory.

Finally, the Tai-Chi system in the book of *I-Ching* shows that it is not only a useful binary system for computer science development in our time, but a cosmological and philosophical system based upon higher mathematics, the principles of relativity, and the quantum physics. Yin and Yang are relative, and they complement and balance each other in the Oneness (太極).

This is an arrangement of the original sixty-four hexagrams, which was showed to Mr. Leibnitz in the seventeenth century by Father Joachim Bouvet, a Jesuit missionary in China.[18]

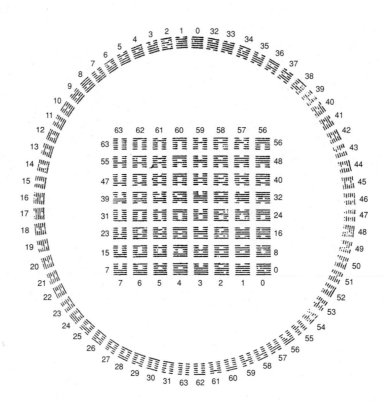

Manageable Pattern of Excess Solar and Lunar Forces on Earth.
All dates are according to the lunar calendar.

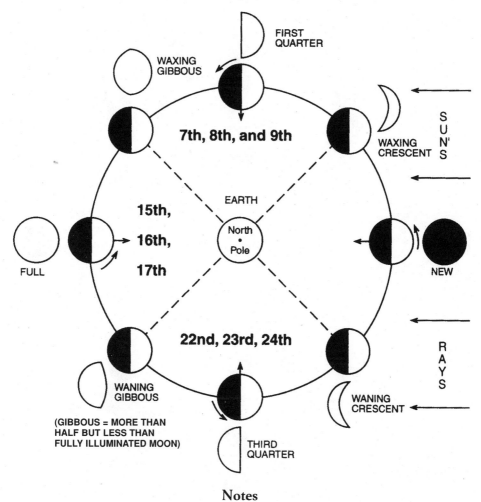

Notes

- *On earth, at certain periods of time, there are patterns of excess Lunar and/or Solar gravitational/centrifugal forces.*
- *In those time periods (see dates on lunar calendar above), these forces have varying degrees of influence on human life.*
- *Especially for those who suffer from cardiovascular, brain, or blood vessel diseases, and for some older people, these forces can bring on sickness and even induce sudden death.*
- *Therefore, during those particular periods of time people should learn how to wisely use these patterns to their advantage; in other words, people should pay special attention to take good care of themselves: to avoid stress, to refrain from drinking liquor, to cultivate good health, and sometimes to adjust their work schedule.[19]*

要掌握太陽月亮吸引力 變化

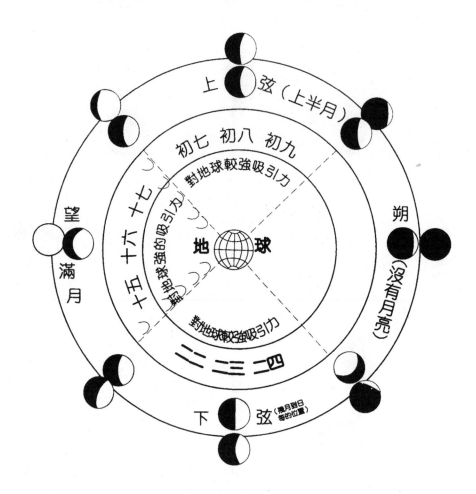

1. 月亮和太陽每月有個時間對地球形成強和較強吸引力.

2. 在這几個日子, 月亮和太陽的吸引力. 對人的生老病死都會
   產生不同程度影嚮.

3. 對于心腦血管病患者和有些老人就可能突然發病, 甚至瘁死.

4. 要掌握太陽和月亮吸引力變化的規律. 在月亮強吸引力期間. 要特別
   注意保持心境平穩, 避免勞累, 不過與飲酒. 恰當調想工作,
   生活節律. 做好自我保健.

伏羲 *Fu-Hsi.*

Mural of Fu-Hsi observing nature from atop the mountain, in
Ten Sui City, Jiangsu Province.

Chang Tao-ling, founder of Taoism, is shown wearing Taoist vestments and riding a tiger (taming the demonic). The tablet in his hands makes him a "civil official of the Way" (tao-shih). This portrait is hung in the southeast corner of the (outer) altar above a table called the Dragon-Tiger Mountain (Lung-hu shan), hereditary home of the Heavenly Masters, of whom Chang is the first.[20]

The Heavenly Worthy of the Way and Its Power, also known as Lord Lao or Lao-tzu (Old Infant). His yellow robe links him to the central element, earth. His Taoist crown and flame recall his revelation to Chang Tao-ling of the Unique Energy by which the Taoist priest "lights the internal burner" and then, by "exteriorizing" this energy, communicates with heaven.

頹隳自甘，
家道難成。

朱子格言

If you allow yourself to become lazy and fall prey to procrastination,
you will not find harmony in your family.
Your inner vitality cannot be awakened and you will get nowhere.[21]

儒家思想 佛教 道教 武術

Confucianism, Buddhism, Taoism, and Wu-Shu

Dan Wang

Wu-Shu or martial arts is a general term for about 360 systematized physical action systems. They range from the unarmed/armed fighting-to-death physical actions to the modern performing combat system of art and science. The latter includes the finest form of *wu-shu,* the Scienceless Science and Artless Art, created to complement an advanced degree of mental power.

This finest form of *wu-shu* is a slow but sure-to-come achievement. Once achieved, it is not only enlightening and stimulating but fascinating and powerful. Learning and refining the complex physical technique and movement alone is not enough. The work must transcend to a degree so advanced that the art becomes an artless art and the science becomes a scienceless science, growing out of the unconscious in a natural, instinctive way. Lightning strikes so thunder booms; the wind blows and the tree bends. *Wu-Shu* is not "copyrighted" but is available to anyone willing to make the commitment to learn.

The lasting and extraordinary contributions of Confucianism, Buddhism, and Taoism to *wu-shu* are the following.

Confucianism — Created an open system of self-actualization for interested learners.

Confucius (551–479 B.C.E.) was the greatest of all Chinese philosophers to arise out of centuries of revolutionary instability and excessive treachery during the Warring States Period in Chinese history. He created and taught Chinese scholars a systematic approach to self-actualization:

A. (定)	Concentration,	
B. (靜)	Calmness, and	
C. (安)	Inner Peace enable	
D. (慮)	Deep Thinking for	
E. (得)	Obtaining Goals —	
F. (修身)	Self-enlightenment,	
G. (齊家)	Family Harmony,	
H. (治國)	National Supervision, and	
I. (平天下)	A United World.	

It was, and still is, a good system for those who want to achieve self-enlightenment. For further study one can research the Chinese classics and interpretations on the subject.

Buddhism — Emphasis on Chan and Chi for Wu-Shu

"The incomparable doctrine of True Buddhism can be understood only after long, hard discipline and by enduring what is most difficult to endure, and by practicing what is most difficult to practice. Men of inferior virtue and wisdom will not comprehend it. All their labors will come to nothing," Bodhidharma told his first disciple.[22]

Bodhidharma (448–527 C.E.) was the third son of a Brahman king. With missionary zeal to spread the Buddhist faith, he left his monastery in Southern India and managed to walk across the treacherous and freezing Himalayan Mountains. He reached the Shao-Lin Temple (Young Forest Temple), which was renowned as a site where scholars translated Buddhist scriptures into Chinese. Upon Bodhidharma's arrival, the head monk, fearing his presence would be disruptive, directed him to remain outside the temple. Determined to stay, Bodhidharma took refuge in a nearby cave to sit in cross-legged meditation facing a rock cliff. For ten years he remained there in absolute silence. A "*Chan* setting" like this was a great help to those who encountered insurmountable obstacles. *Chan* is the perception of self-nature. Enlightenment and salvation can only be achieved by inward understanding and such illumination cannot be outwardly communicated. At the time, his philosophy of silence aimed to "put an end to the formation of all external relationships and be rid of any strong and fierce internal desires; then, and only then, with a mind like a wall, indifferent to outside disruption, he enters into the truth."[23]

Once, during meditation, sleep overcame Bodhidharma. This so offended his profound sense of discipline that when he awoke, he cut himself as punishment.

At the end of ten years, the wall-gazing Brahman could hear the screeching of ants crawling along the face of the rock. And his large, deep-blue, piercing eyes with a powerful steady gaze had drilled a gaping hole in the cliff wall.

After seeing Bodhidharma's power, the stunned Shao-Lin head monk could no longer resist his obviously superior authority. Thus, Bodhidharma entered the Shao-Lin Monastery main gate to become the first Grand Master, Ta-Mo-Lao-Tsu, of the *Chan* sect in China.

When he saw his monks napping or drowsy during the vital meditation exercises, Bodhiharma realized that their weak bodies could not stand the demand of prolonged mental discipline.

Although Buddhism is aimed specifically at the salvation of the mind, Bodhidharma explained to the monks that body and mind are inseparable. This unity must be maintained for enlightenment. With the idea of physically inspiring his monks to greater spiritual heights, Bodhidharma introduced systematized exercises to strengthen the body and mind for health and self-defense purposes.

The emphasis on *chi* is another of Bodhidharma's contributions to the artless art and scienceless science of empty-hand combat techniques.

The cultivation of *chi*, the vital energy flow, was Bodhidharma's primary concern in meditation. He emphasized the acquisition of control over this internal force and the use of its power to mold superior human beings. "Breath" is the flywheel of life, based on respiration. But the flow of the *chi* starts from the feet, develops in the legs, is directed by waist, moves up to the spine, then to the arms, hands, and fingers. These are the channels of the flow of *chi*. When the *chi* is well-channeled, the whole body becomes alive, and when the *chi* is released, the whole body becomes one unit in action.

Taoism — Focuses on the balance of Yin/Yang and Relativity

The most influential spiritual sect in China after the Confucians were the Taoists, who directed their teaching toward the individual search for a higher form of physical and mental existence. Their most important contribution to the Chinese *wu-shu* has been the creation of Tai-Chi Chuan, a complete balance and muscular control system initially designed to maintain health, calm the mind, and increase longevity. Self-defense methods were devised later for highly advanced states of training.

Tai-Chi Chuan is based on Tai-Chi Tao, a dynamic tranquility residing in a state of nothingness. Both Taoism and Buddhism teach us to live in harmony with nature. Through Tai-Chi we learn that we are halves of a whole, segments of a beautiful universe, and not adversaries caught in a vicious circle. It is not "cosmic unity" but our true selves. Sometimes life is like a stage show. Yet we must never forget to return to our natural selves when the stage curtain falls.

Tai-Chi Chuan is the combination of inner experience and outer performance. People who have practiced Tai-Chi Chuan for a long time will develop the following characteristics. They are usually cheerful, trusting, compassionate, generous, patient, and alert. They complain very little. They find pleasure in ordinary and simple things. These qualities can become a part of us if we permit Tai-Chi Chuan to help us formulate them.

Developing in line with philosophy, science, theory, thought, mathematics, and the laws of nature, *wu-shu* or martial arts includes Shao-Lin Chuan, Pa-Kua Tsang, Shing-Yi Chuan, and Tai-

Chi Chuan. They evolved through the centuries and most of them incorporated aspects of Taoism, Buddhism, and Confucianism into their combat systems. Their intention is to help students intuitively understand important truths, and to expand their insight and potential rather than simply intellectualize these ideas.

In addition to all the above, in order to achieve victory in combat, you must place yourself in your opponent's shoes:

If you don't understand your true self, you will lose 100 percent of the time;

If you do understand your true self, you will win 50 percent of the time;

If you understand both your own and your opponent's true selves, you will win 100 percent of the time.

至聖先師

孔夫子 Confucius

二四　學琴師襄

孔子向師襄
學習彈琴，十日
不更換曲子，襄
子勸他練習別的
曲子，孔子以還
沒有掌握此曲道
理而推辭。以後
襄子又先後兩次
觀他，他又分別
以沒有了解此曲
志向、為人作理
由而推辭。後來
才知此曲是相傳
周文王所作的琴
曲
見《史記·孔子
世家》、《孔子家
語·辯樂》。《文王操》（事

Learning to Play Music from Shixiang [24]

Confucius learned to play musical instruments from Master Xiang. He played the same piece of music for ten days. Then Master Xiang advised him to change to something else. Confucius reasoned that he had not understood the meaning behind it, so he kept on. Afterwards, Scholar Xiang persuaded him twice to change the music, yet twice he refused by saying that he had not gotten the aspiration and moral of it. And it turned out later that the music had been composed by King Wen of Zhou. [25]

佛 教
Buddhism

Amitofuo in mediation. Sifu Kuo Lien-Ying meditated daily at 4:00 a.m. in this way for fifteen minutes to promote calmness and concentration.[26]

佛 教
Buddhism

Image of Buddha in heaven from Malaysia.

南無釋迦牟尼佛 *Shakyamuni Buddha with students.*

Traditional Chinese image of female Buddha,
Kwan Yin Pusa.

觀世音菩薩 *Kuan Say Im Phor Sart*

When drinking the water, remember the source;
Honor those from whom our blessings flow.[27]
—Confucius

Chan (Meditation)

*The author's mother Hung-Lan (Buddhist name),
A-Hsiang W. Lu (given name).*

修心養性

禪

Chan strengthens body and mind.[28]

Hua-Tu
The Great Physician

Hua-Tu was born in An-Hwei province in 141 C.E. Before he died in 203 C.E. he became a famous scholar and doctor in China. He specialized in the field of surgery. He possessed a great knowledge of acupuncture and anesthetics. He refused a government offer to be a high-ranking official, choosing instead to spend his life as a private citizen helping people alleviate their physical ailments and suffering.[29]

The Three King Dynasty (190 C.E.) was so-named because of three famous generals, Kuan Yu (關羽), Liu Bai (劉備), and Zhang Fei (張飛). One of these generals, Kuan Yu, was badly injured and Hua-Tu volunteered to operate on his wounded arm. To take his mind off the agony of the surgery, Hua-Tu used a powerful combination of herbs as an anesthetic.

To maintain good health, Hua-Tu believed, prevention is more important than cure. To this end, he created and taught a form of exercise called the "five-animal system." The animals include the sparrow, deer, monkey, bear, and tiger.

Hua-Tu observed animals to understand their nature and believed that to promote and maintain good health, one must exercise. Hua-Tu was very famous among the Chinese people and remains a hero to this day.

華　佗

Hua-Tu.

五禽戲姿勢圖

Five-Animal System.

Beijing Opera and Chinese Acrobatics

Chinese martial arts have been influential in the development of two related art forms: Beijing Opera and Chinese Acrobatics. Performers of both disciplines receive an intense amount of martial arts training in addition to their specific performance training. Traditionally, performers begin training for these arts at the age of five and train intensively throughout their school years, rising before dawn for demanding sessions of exercise and practice. This may account for these performers' amazing feats of strength, flexibility, and agility.

Beijing Opera is unlike any single Western art form because it intertwines the use of acrobatics and weapons. There is no one word that can describe Beijing Opera; there is no other theatrical or musical experience that can compare. It is a mixture of martial arts, mime, gymnastics, pageantry, ballet, acrobatics, circus, silent movie, and opera. These shows are filled with spectacle, dazzling sights, and exotic sounds, and often tell strange and engrossing stories. These stories, such as the well-known "Monkey King," are taken from both mythology and history, and often include elaborate battle scenes during which martial arts are displayed with enormous energy and skill.

Performers of both arts show that they can do almost anything with their bodies, often defying both gravity and anatomy. Use of weapons and incredible stunts demonstrate the performers' balance, flexibility, and strength in the martial arts. In the famous historical operas, "Battle for Yen Teng Mountain" and "The White Snake," acrobatics play a major role. All of the segments must be perfectly timed and each movement precisely executed, especially when working with other members of the group.

In the majority of the Beijing Opera stories, the males are strong, powerful heroes. However, in "The White Snake," the heroine is a female character who victoriously battles against four males. The skills of the female martial artist are fully displayed in this story. In the world of Beijing Opera, it does not matter whether the performer is male or female. Both are trained and disciplined in exactly the same way to produce an unforgettable performance.

There is another side of Beijing Opera, which is not all spectacle, but intimately, intensely, human, and at times very humorous. All this is achieved without sacrificing its physical virtuosity. Beijing Opera can even laugh at itself, as in the story "The Three-Forked Crossroads" where a would-be hero innkeeper and a traveler battle in the darkness of the traveler's room.

Positions used in Beijing Opera are similar to those of Shao-Lin Chuan.[30]

"Battle for Yen Teng Mountain".

"Monkey King".   *"The Three-Forked Crossroads".*

"The White Snake".

Chinese Beijing Opera.

"Battle for Yen Teng Mountain".

少林拳 *Shao-Lin Chuan*

二狼拳 *Erh-Lang Chuan is advanced Shao-Lin Chuan.*

Chinese Beijing Opera.

Movements in Chinese acrobatics are similiar to those of Shao-Lin Chuan.[31]

舞獅

Lion Dancers.

少林拳 *Shao-Lin Chuan*

查拳 *Tsa-Chuan is advanced Shao-Lin Chuan.*

Chinese acrobatics.

American Conservatory Theater (A.C.T.) San Francisco, 1969.

Martial Arts exercises are also useful for dancers.

郭明利 *Kuo Ming Li, grandson of Sifu Kuo, in China.*

郭中美 *Kuo Chung-Mei, son of Sifu Kuo, in the United States.*

Rope Dart (鏢頭)
This hand weapon is concealed and secured beneath the outer clothing in such a way that it can be hurled within less than a second and retracted, allowing the bodyguard to protect a group of people from a distance. Because of the great skill required for its effective use, in old China only the head bodyguard carried a Rope Dart.

Dispersing Hands (散手)
After practicing the Universal Post Stance 1/2 hour to an hour per standing and putting chin to toe, some lower-body flexibility and upper-body stability are attained. Students may then learn Dispersing Hands, an exercise in self-defense and concentration.

少林拳

Shao-Lin Chuan Tan-Tui

San Francisco State University.

Shao-Lin Chuan, Beijing.

少 林 拳

Students from Beijing Tung County.

Shao-Lin Chuan.

少林拳

Shao-Lin Chuan students from Beijing Tung County.

少 林 趕 棒
SHAO-LIN CHASING BAT

少林單刀
SHAO-LIN SINGLE BROAD-SWORD

太極劍 - 單,雙
TAI-CHI SWORD - SINGLE,DOUBLE

八 卦 掌
BA-QUOK PALM

形 意 拳
SHING-YEE CHUAN

一九七九年六月廿音蓮薩 郭蓮 薩印

安之居

"Harmony in the Home"
Calligraphy by Sifu Kuo.

*Mimi (1976-1994) and Ling-Ling (1983-1992) brought lots
of joy to the Kuo Family and all the students.*

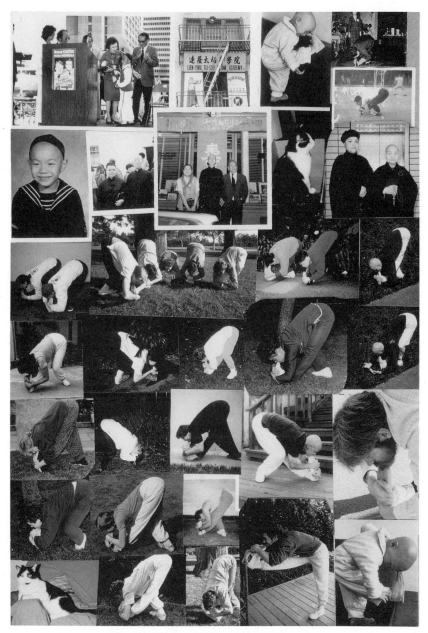

Dedicated students of Sifu and Simu Kuo.

古之學者為己，
今之學者為人。

In the old days, men sought knowledge
in order to improve themselves.
Nowadays, men seek knowledge
to impress other people.
— Confucius [32]

Notes

1. Lien-Ying Kuo, *Tai-Chi Chuan Rhythm* (Taipei: self-published, 1963). Calligraphy by his student, Dr. Lee Yok-Ying.

2. Taken from a scroll on the wall at Confucius Temple, Shang-Ding Village in Zouyi, state of Lu. Poet unknown. English translation by Rong-Chong Chen, Ph.D.

3. Wu Juntao, and Ni Peiling, eds., *300 Tang Poems: A New Translation* (Hong Kong: Business Publishing Co., 1987). Poem by Wang Zhihuan, translation by Xu Yuan-Zhong.

4. Unpublished poem by Yao You-Wei. Translation by Rong-Chong Chen, Ph.D.

5. Chin Chung Tsai, ed., *Da Xue: The Great Learning* (Singapore: Asiapac, 1992). Poet unknown, trans. Mary Ng En Tzu.

6. Chin Chung Tsai, ed., *Lu Yu: The Analects,* trans. Mary Ng En Tzu (Singapore: Asiapac, 1992), p. 51.

7. Chin Chung Tsai, ed., *Zhong Yong: The Doctrine of the Mean,* trans. Mary Ng En Tzu (Singapore: Asiapac, 1992), p. 51.

8. Lien-Ying Kuo, op. cit. Calligraphy by his student Dr. Sen Tsang-Huan.

9. This poem is from the "Classic of Tai-Chi Chuan" as it appears in Lien-Ying Kuo, op. cit.

10. Photo by Richard Grosse.

11. A common poem, known to all Chinese people.

12. This is the earliest arrangement that is attributed to Fu-Hsi. Note the dynamic actions of opposites or the law of polar reversal. For further information, please see R. L. Wing, *The Illustrated I-Ching* (Garden City, New York: Doubleday & Company, 1982).

13. The Fu-Hsi sequence (26=64 hexagrams) was the very arrangement that led the seventeenth-century father of calculus, G. W. Leibnitz, to the discovery of the binary number system used in our time. A Jesuit priest in China at the time, Father Joachim Bouvet, showed this sequence to Leibnitz, a German philosopher and mathematician (1646–1716), who was astonished to discover that this was none other than the binary notation for numbers 0 through 63.

14. See Wing, op. cit., pp. 12-14.

15. Martin Gardner, "Mathematical Games," *Scientific American,* January, 1974.

16. Ibid.

17. Joseph Needham, *Science and Civilization in China,* Vol. 2 (Cambridge, Massachusetts: Cambridge University Press, 1969), p. 505.

18. See note 14.

19. This information comes from the author's personal experience and research.

20. This plate and the one on the following page are both from John Lagerwey, *Taoist Ritual in Chinese Society and History* (New York: Macmillan Publishing Co., 1987). Used by permission.

21. Martin Palmer, ed., *T'ung Shu: The Ancient Chinese Almanac* (Malaysia: Vinpress, 1986). Poem by Zhu Zi. Translation by Dan Wang.

22. Ruth Sasaki, *Zen Dust* (New York: Harcourt, Brace and World, 1966).

23. Ibid.

24. Left: *China Reconstructs,* Vol. XXXVIII, No. 9, September 1989 (Beijing: China Welfare Institute). Cover illustration, artist unknown. Right: Kouson Lu, ed., *The Pictures about Confucius' Life,* trans. Ma Shu-Ching, (Jinan, China: Shandong Friendship Press, 1989). Under the Qufu Administration Commission of the Cultural Relics of Shandong.

25. Alan W. Watts and Mary Jane Watts, *The Way of Zen* (New York: Vintage Books, 1957, 1985).

26. This plate and those on the following two pages are from the collection of Hung-Lan, the author's mother. Materials given away by the Tsu Guong Buddhist Temple. The poem in calligraphy reads: "Tolerating somebody shows the high morals of oneself. Bullying nobody makes oneself feel fully at ease." The painting and calligraphy are by Prof. Yao You-Wei. English translation by Jin Yu.

27. A common poem, known to all Chinese people.

28. Buddhist quote provided by Hung-Lan.

29. San Huang Lan Pui, *Chinese Medicine Development History* (Hong Kong: Shian-Lee Publishing Co., 1974), p. 89.

30. Photographs of the Beijing Opera on this and the following pages are from program notes. Taiwan, 1978 and Beijing, 1981.

31. Photos of Chinese acrobatics on this and the following page are from Hong-Jun Lu and Song Shufa, *Secrets of Shaolin Gongfu,* trans. Quo Zheng-Ji, Beijing Slide Studio.
32. Chin Chung Tsai, ed., *The Analects,* trans. Mary Ng En Tzu (Singapore: Asiapac, 1992), p. 50.